LAW, CRIME AND LAW ENFORCEMENT

CORPORATE CRIMINAL LIABILITY

FEDERAL LAW AND PROSECUTORIAL DISCRETION ISSUES

LAW, CRIME AND LAW ENFORCEMENT

Additional books in this series can be found on Nova's website
under the Series tab.

Additional e-books in this series can be found on Nova's website
under the e-book tab.

LAW, CRIME AND LAW ENFORCEMENT

CORPORATE CRIMINAL LIABILITY

FEDERAL LAW AND PROSECUTORIAL DISCRETION ISSUES

BRANDON P. BURTON
EDITOR

NOVINKA

New York

For permission to use material from this book please contact us:
Telephone 631-231-7269; Fax 631-231-8175
Web Site: http://www.novapublishers.com

Library of Congress Cataloging-in-Publication Data

ISBN: 978-1-63117-724-8

Published by Nova Science Publishers, Inc. † New York

CONTENTS

Preface		**vii**
Chapter 1	Corporate Criminal Liability: An Overview of Federal Law *Charles Doyle*	**1**
Chapter 2	Prosecutorial Discretion in the Context of Corporate Attorney-Client Relations *Charles Doyle*	**41**
Index		**83**

PREFACE

Individual criminal statutes, Justice Department policies, and the Sentencing Guidelines largely dictate the circumstances under which, and the extent to which, agents, employees, corporations, and similar unincorporated entities are prosecuted and punished. This book provides a brief overview of federal law in the area. This book also provides a brief discussion of the legislation, the legal background, and a chronology of related issues and events.

Chapter 1 – A corporation is criminally liable for the federal crimes its employees or agents commit in its interest. Corporate officers, employees, and agents are individually liable for the crimes they commit, for the crimes they conspire to commit, for the foreseeable crimes their coconspirators commit, for the crimes whose commission they aid and abet, and for the crimes whose perpetrators they assist after the fact.

The decision whether to prosecute a corporation rests with the Justice Department. Internal guidelines identify the factors that are to be weighed: the strength of the case against the corporation; the extent and history of misconduct; the existence of a compliance program; the corporation's cooperation with the investigation; the collateral consequences; whether the corporation has made restitution or taken other remedial measures; and the alternatives to federal prosecution. As in the case of individual defendants, corporation prosecutions rarely result in a criminal trial. More often, the corporation pleads guilty or enters into a deferred or delayed prosecution agreement.

Chapter 2 – The Justice Department enjoys prosecutorial discretion to bring criminal charges against a corporation, its culpable officers or employees, or both. For a corporation, indictment alone can be catastrophic, if not fatal, in some instances. The Thompson Memorandum, since replaced with guidelines in the U. S. Attorneys Manual, described the policy factors to be considered in the exercise of prosecutorial discretion. Two of the factors explicitly mentioned were whether a corporation had waived its privileges and whether it had cut off the payment of attorneys' fees for its officers and employees.

Justice Department policies and practices under the Thompson Memorandum led to constitutional challenges based on the Fifth Amendment's self-incrimination clause, the Amendment's due process clause, and the Sixth Amendment's right to counsel clause. Due process and right to counsel concerns were enough for a federal district court in New York to throw out the indictments of thirteen former partners and employees of an accounting firm, charged with creating and marketing fraudulent tax shelters, *United States v. Stein.* The Second Circuit affirmed on right to counsel grounds and consequently found it necessary to address the merits of the due process argument.

In: Corporate Criminal Liability
Editor: Brandon P. Burton
ISBN: 978-1-63117-724-8

Chapter 1

CORPORATE CRIMINAL LIABILITY: AN OVERVIEW OF FEDERAL LAW*

Charles Doyle

SUMMARY

A corporation is criminally liable for the federal crimes its employees or agents commit in its interest. Corporate officers, employees, and agents are individually liable for the crimes they commit, for the crimes they conspire to commit, for the foreseeable crimes their coconspirators commit, for the crimes whose commission they aid and abet, and for the crimes whose perpetrators they assist after the fact.

The decision whether to prosecute a corporation rests with the Justice Department. Internal guidelines identify the factors that are to be weighed: the strength of the case against the corporation; the extent and history of misconduct; the existence of a compliance program; the corporation's cooperation with the investigation; the collateral consequences; whether the corporation has made restitution or taken other remedial measures; and the alternatives to federal prosecution. As in the case of individual defendants, corporation prosecutions rarely result in a criminal trial. More often, the

* This is an edited, reformatted and augmented version of a Congressional Research Service publication, CRS Report for Congress R43293, dated October 30, 2013.

corporation pleads guilty or enters into a deferred or delayed prosecution agreement.

During a criminal investigation and throughout the course of criminal proceedings, corporations enjoy many, but not all, of the constitutional rights implicated in the criminal investigation or prosecution of an individual. Corporations have no Fifth Amendment privilege against self-incrimination. On the other hand, the courts have recognized or have assumed that corporations have a First Amendment right to free speech; a Fourth Amendment protection against unreasonable searches and seizures; a Fifth Amendment right to due process and protection against double jeopardy; Sixth Amendment rights to counsel, jury trial, speedy trial, and to confront accusers, and to subpoena witnesses; and Eighth Amendment protection against excessive fines.

Corporations cannot be jailed. Otherwise, corporations and individuals face many of the same consequences following conviction. The federal Sentencing Guidelines influence the sentencing consequences of conviction in many instances. Corporations can be fined. They can be placed on probation. They can be ordered to pay restitution. Their property can be confiscated. They can be barred from engaging in various types of commercial activity. The Guidelines speak to all of these.

For example, the corporate fine Guidelines begin with the premise that a totally corrupt corporation should be fined out of existence, if the statutory maximum permits. A corporation operated for criminal purposes or by criminal means should be fined at a level sufficient to strip it of all of its assets. In other cases, the Guidelines recommend fines and other sentencing features that reflect the nature and seriousness of the crime of conviction and the level of corporate culpability.

INTRODUCTION

Under federal law, corporations or most other legal entities may be criminally liable for the crimes of their employees and agents.[1] This is true in the case of regulatory offenses, like crimes in violation of the Federal Food, Drug, and Cosmetic Act; it is true in the case of economic offenses, like crimes in violation of the securities laws; and it is true in the case of common law crimes, like keeping a house of prostitution in violation of the Mann Act. Ordinarily, the agents and employees who commit the crimes for which their principals and employers are liable also face prosecution and punishment.

Individual criminal statutes, Justice Department policies, and the Sentencing Guidelines largely dictate the circumstances under which, and the extent to which, agents, employees, corporations, and similar unincorporated entities are prosecuted and punished. This is a brief overview of federal law in the area.

BACKGROUND

It was said at common law that "a corporation cannot commit treason, or felony, or other crime, in its corporate capacity: though its members may, in their distinct individual capacities."[2] That perception changed over time. First, it was agreed that a corporation might be held criminally liable for its failure to honor certain legal obligations (nonfeasance);[3] then for the inadequate manner in which it performed certain legal obligations (malfeasance).[4] At the dawn of the 20th century, the Supreme Court expressed a more sweeping view:

> It is true that there are some crimes which, in their nature, cannot be committed by corporations. But there is a large class of offenses ... wherein the crime consists in purposely doing the things prohibited by statute. In that class of crimes we see no good reason why corporations may not be held responsible for and charged with the knowledge and purposes of their agents, acting within the authority conferred upon them. If it were not so, many offenses might go unpunished and acts be committed in violation of law where, as in the present case, the statute requires all persons, corporate or private, to refrain from certain practices, forbidden in the interest of public policy.[5]

The Court spoke of "crimes which in their nature, cannot be committed by corporations," but did not explain what specific crimes it had in mind. When it spoke, it did so in the midst of a debate over whether a corporation could be held criminally liable not only for crimes of action and inaction (malfeasance and nonfeasance) of its agents but also for those crimes which required that their agents acted with a specific intent (mens rea) such as the intent to defraud ("since a corporation has no soul, it cannot have actual wicked intent").[6]

The Court pointed toward resolution of the issue, however, when it observed that the question turns on the nature of the crime and not the nature of the corporation ("some crimes in their nature, cannot be committed by corporations"). Since, in the federal sphere, there is no crime but by act of

Congress, the question is one of statutory proscription and congressional intent.

ENTITIES SUBJECT TO CORPORATE CRIMINAL LIABILITY

Most federal criminal statutes apply to "whoever," or to any "person" who violates their prohibitions. Although, in ordinary parlance, the word "person" usually refers to a human being, the law often gives it a broader meaning.[7] The Dictionary Act provides that "In determining the meaning of any Act of Congress, unless the context indicates otherwise ... the words 'person' or 'whoever' include corporations, companies, associations, firms, partnerships, societies, and joint stock companies, as well as individuals."[8] The courts have used the Dictionary Act definition to give meaning to the words "person" or "whoever" in the context of a criminal statute.[9]

Federal statutes frequently provide individual definitions of the entities that fall within their proscriptions. Some are as terse as that of the racketeering statute, "'person' includes any individual or entity capable of holding a legal or beneficial interest in property."[10] Others, like the tax crime definition, are more detailed:

> When used in this title, where not otherwise distinctly expressed or manifestly incompatible with the intent thereof—(1) Person.-The term "person" shall be construed to mean and include an individual, a trust, estate, partnership, association, company or corporation. (2) Partnership and partner.-The term "partnership" includes a syndicate, group, pool, joint venture, or other unincorporated organization, through or by means of which any business, financial operation, or venture is carried on, and which is not, within the meaning of this title, a trust or estate or a corporation; and the term "partner" includes a member in such a syndicate, group, pool, joint venture, or organization. (3) Corporation.-The term "corporation" includes associations, joint-stock companies, and insurance companies.[11]

Still others have taken special care to mention governmental entities when listing those covered by their proscriptions.[12] The caution reflects judicial reluctance, absent explicit language, to conclude that Congress intends to expose governmental entities to punitive measures.[13]

SCOPE OF AUTHORITY

In federal law, corporate criminal liability is ordinarily confined to offenses (a) committed by the corporation's officers, employees, or agents; (b) within the scope of their employment; and (c) at least in part for the benefit of the corporation.[14] The test for whether an activity falls within the individual's scope of authority is whether the individual engages in activities "on the corporation's behalf in performance of [his] general line of work.... those acts must be motivated, at least in part, by an intent to benefit the corporation."[15] If the standard is met, the corporation will be liable notwithstanding the fact that it expressly directed its agent, employee, or officer not to commit the offense at issue.[16]

Under the Model Penal Code[17] and many state penal codes, corporate criminal liability may depend upon the misconduct of senior management officials; the misconduct of lower level employees is not always enough even when they act within their scope of authority for the corporation's benefit.[18]

IMPUTED INTENT AND KNOWLEDGE

As a general rule, "[c]orporations may be held liable for the specific intent offenses based on the 'knowledge and intent' of their employees."[19] Again, the rule extends only to those instances when the employee or agent acted, or acquired knowledge, within the scope of his or her employment, seeking, at least in part, to benefit the corporation.[20] The law is somewhat more uncertain when a corporation's liability turns not upon the knowledge or the intent of a single employee but upon cumulative actions or knowledge of several.[21]

LIABILITY OF OFFICERS, EMPLOYEES, AGENTS, ACCOMPLICES, AND CONSPIRATORS

With rare exception, statutes which expose a corporation to criminal liability do not absolve the officers, employees, or agents whose violations are responsible for the corporation's plight. From time to time, the courts have encountered the argument that an individual cannot be at once both the person who violates the statute and the personification of the corporation that violates the statute: "[W]hen the officer is acting solely for his corporation, the appellee contends that he is no longer a 'person' within the Act. The rationale for this distinction is that the activities of the officer, however illegal and culpable, are chargeable to the corporation as the principal but not to the individual who perpetrates them."[22] To which the courts have responded, "No intent to exculpate a corporate officer who violates the law is to be imputed to Congress without clear compulsion."[23]

Conspiracy raises a slightly more difficult issue. Conspiracy is the agreement of two or more persons to commit some other federal crime.[24] Although the courts have sometimes recognized an intracorporate defense in civil conspiracy cases, they have concluded that a corporation and each of the participating individuals may be liable for plots among two or more of the corporation's officers or employees.[25] On the other hand, a "corporate officer, acting alone on behalf of the corporation, [may] not be convicted of conspiring with the corporation."[26]

Conspiracy also presents one of the three situations in which corporate officials and employees may face criminal liability under federal law even though they themselves did not commit, and perhaps did not even know of, the misconduct of other officers or employees. Thus, though an officer or employee has no direct hand in the matter, he is liable for foreseeable offenses committed by one of his co-conspirators in furtherance of their common scheme.[27]

The second situation occurs when the official or employee either instructs another to commit a federal offense or aids and abets another in the commission of a federal offense, or takes some action after the fact to conceal the commission of a federal offense by another. Like conspiracy, liability for procuring or aiding and abetting the offense of another focuses on conduct committed before the commission of the underlying substantive offense:

> Whoever commits an offense against the United States or aids, abets, counsels, commands, induces or procures its commission, is punishable as a principal. (b) Whoever willfully causes an act to be done which if directly performed by him or another would be an offense against the United States, is punishable as a principal.[28]

"In order to aid and abet another to commit a crime it is necessary that a defendant in some sort associate himself with the venture, that he participate in it as in something that he wishes to bring about, that he seek by his action to make it succeed."[29] The officer or employee must know of the colleague's pending misconduct and by his action intend to facilitate it.[30] Moreover, unlike conspiracy, which requires at least two individuals, even a sole stockholder may be guilty of aiding and abetting the crime of a corporation.[31]

Misprision and liability as an accessory after the fact focus on conduct committed after the commission of the underlying substantive offense.[32] Misprision requires proof that the defendant knew of the commission of a federal felony by another, and that he not only failed to report the offense to authorities but affirmatively acted to conceal it.[33] An accessory after the fact charge requires proof that the defendant knew of the commission of a federal offense by another and assisted the other to avoid arrest, trial or punishment.[34] Both statutes essentially create general obstruction of justice offenses. Consequently, the specific actions which offend their prohibitions will often constitute offenses under other more specific federal obstruction statutes.[35]

The third instance of official liability triggered by the misconduct of others within the corporation requires no knowing participation, but instead occurs when a corporate official, responsible to do so, fails to prevent the commission of an offense. This is the least common of the three. It arises in the context of a regulatory scheme, crafted to ensure public welfare and capped with a criminal proscription which says nothing of the knowledge necessary for conviction. Two Supreme Court cases under the Federal Food, Drug, and Cosmetic Act first brought to prominence this so-called "responsible corporate official" doctrine.[36]

The doctrine is triggered by legislation "of a now familiar type which dispenses with the conventional requirement of criminal conduct-awareness for some wrongdoing. In the interest of the larger good it puts the burden of acting at hazard upon a person otherwise innocent but standing in responsible relation to a public danger."[37] The legislation generally involves the regulation of "potentially harmful or injurious items."[38] "In such situations," the courts "have reasoned that as long as a defendant knows that he is dealing with a dangerous device of a character that places him in responsible relation to a public danger, he should be alerted to the probability of strict regulation,"[39] And they have further "assumed that in such cases Congress intended to place the burden on the defendant to 'ascertain at his peril whether his conduct comes within the inhibition of the statute.'"[40] Thus, they "essentially have relied on the nature of the statute and the particular character of the items regulated to determine whether congressional silence concerning the mental element of the offense should be interpreted as dispensing with conventional *mens rea* requirements."[41]

In such a legislative setting, "the Government establishes a prima facie case when it introduces evidence sufficient to warrant a finding by the trier of the facts that the defendant had, by reason of his position in the corporation, responsibility and authority either to prevent in the first instance, or promptly to correct, the violation complained of, and that he failed to do so."[42]

PROSECUTORIAL DISCRETION

Generally

The decision to prosecute a corporation or its culpable employees or both is vested in the Justice Department.[43] The courts will review the exercise of that discretion only in rare instances and then primarily to protect the constitutional rights of a defendant or potential defendant.[44]

The Justice Department has two sets of guidelines governing the decision to prosecute—one general ("Principles of Federal Prosecution") and the other a supplement devoted to corporations ("Principles of Federal Prosecution of Business Organizations").[45] As they make clear, the decision to prosecute is in fact a series of decisions. The first is whether to initiate, decline, or defer a prosecution. Here perhaps the most easily assessed factor is the strength of the case against the defendant or defendants. Prosecutors ordinarily will not initiate a prosecution unless there is probable cause to believe that a person has committed a federal crime.[46]

On the other hand, prosecutors will seriously consider initiating a prosecution if they believe that they have sufficient admissible evidence to secure a conviction.[47] In those instances, the additional factors that influence the determination to prosecute fall into three categories: the weight of the federal interest, the prospect of effective prosecution elsewhere; and the adequacy of other alternatives.[48]

Federal Interests

Whether to proceed with a prosecutable case ordinarily turns on the nature and seriousness of the offense and the culpability of the defendants. Some crimes, such as those involving immigration civil rights, or federal tax violations, may warrant federal prosecution because of their very nature. Others, such as those involving major fraud or illicit drug trafficking, may call for federal prosecution because of the wide-spread harm they can inflict. The critical factors when it comes to corporate liability, however, are culpability factors. The factors identified in the business organization guidelines include

- pervasiveness of the wrongdoing within the corporation;[49]
- the corporation's history of misconduct;[50]
- the existence and performance of compliance programs;[51]
- the corporation's timely and voluntary disclosure of wrongdoing;[52]
- the corporation's cooperation;[53]
- absence of obstruction;[54]
- collateral consequences;[55]
- restitution.[56]

Pervasiveness

The question is, was the corporation the victim of a rogue employee or is it a rogue corporation? Is crime committed for the corporation's benefit condemned, tolerated, or encouraged? Is the crime the work of an isolated individual or does corruption permeate the corporation? "Charging a corporation for even minor misconduct may be appropriate where the wrongdoing was pervasive and was undertaken by a large number of employees, or by all the employees in a particular role within the corporation, or was condoned by upper management."[57] Conversely, it may not be appropriate to charge a corporation, "particularly one with a robust compliance program in place, under a strict *respondeat superior* theory for the single isolated act of a rogue employee."[58] Most cases will fall between the two extremes and require recourse to other factors as well.

Corporate History

One indication of the pervasiveness of corruption within a corporation may be its involvement and response to any wrongdoing in its past. Past criminal conduct is telling, but the guidelines explain that earlier civil or regulatory enforcement actions may also be taken into account.[59] The same may be said of the past transgressions of subsidiaries or affiliates, although short of a corporate department for the commission of criminal offenses the presence of subsidiaries or other liability-limiting features of corporate structure are not considered dispositive.[60]

Compliance Programs

As noted earlier, a corporation may be liable for employee misconduct even where it has warned its employees against committing the offense.[61]

However, both the guidelines and the U.S. Sentencing Commission's Sentencing Guidelines encourage compliance programs.[62] While a mere "paper program" may be to little avail, a closely supervised, widely dispersed compliance program tailored to detect and prevent the offenses most likely to occur in the corporation's operational environment may have a real impact. An effective plan may reduce the chances of a prosecution and reduce the severity of the charges and any subsequent sentence should a prosecution occur.[63]

Cooperation

The cooperative aspects of the guidelines are among its most controversial attributes. It may be thought unseemly for a corporation to profit from the misdeeds of an employee and then escape liability by turning its benefactor over to the authorities. Moreover, the lines between rewarding cooperation and punishing the assertion of constitutional and other legal rights are not easily drawn. The guidelines point out that the Justice "Department encourages corporations, as part of their compliance programs, to conduct internal investigations and to disclose the relevant facts to the appropriate authorities."[64] This is only one of the guideline's cooperation directives. A second is the reminder that cooperation alone does not necessarily shield a corporation from prosecution.[65] Earlier Justice Department policies relating to corporate cooperation with federal prosecutors came under fire because of concerns that they might interfere with the Sixth Amendment rights of corporations and corporate officials.[66]

The guidelines now seek to still those concerns by emphasizing that "[w]hat the government seeks and needs to advance its legitimate (indeed, essential) law enforcement mission is not waiver of those [attorney-client and attorney work product] protections, but rather the facts known to the corporation about the putative criminal misconduct under review. In addition, while a corporation remains free to convey non-factual or 'core' attorney-client communications or work product—if and only if the corporation voluntarily chooses to do so—prosecutors should not ask for such waivers and are directed not to do so."[67] By the same token, while corporate officials are not free to obstruct an investigation, the mere fact that a corporation pays the attorneys' fees of its officers or employees or enters into joint defense agreements will ordinarily not constitute obstruction.[68] Attorneys who feel a prosecutor has breached these assurances are encouraged to contact senior Justice Department officials.[69]

A corporation may also receive credit for agreeing to make victim restitution, disciplining offending employees, or addressing short-comings in its compliance program.[70] Finally, a prosecutor may consider the adverse impact of a prosecution on innocent employees or shareholders.[71]

Prosecution Elsewhere

The general guidelines remind prosecutors that prosecution in another jurisdiction may be more advantageous, particularly when the interests of the other jurisdiction are comparatively more substantial or the prospects of a more appropriate sentence are greater.[72]

Alternatives to Criminal Trial

Prosecutors have several alternatives to criminal trial. They may accept a corporation's offer to plead guilty. They may defer prosecution of the corporation under a deferred prosecution agreement. They may accept a corporation's offer to sign a non-prosecution agreement, frequently with the intent to prosecute corporate officials or employees. They may elect to forgo prosecution in favor of civil sanctions.

Finally, since corporate misconduct often occurs in a regulatory context, civil or regulatory sanctions may be available. Whether prosecutors consider them appealing alternatives may depend in part on the severity of the misconduct and the severity of the sanctions. The factors the guidelines identify include "the strength of the regulatory authority's interest; the regulatory authority's ability and willingness to take effective enforcement action; and the probable sanction if the regulatory authority's enforcement action is upheld."[73]

Deferred and Non-prosecution Agreements

The common perception is that the announcement of its indictment sounds a large corporation's death knell.[74] Consequently, a large corporation, threatened with the prospect of indictment, may be inclined to accept a deferred prosecution agreement or a non-prosecution agreement at terms particularly favorable to the government.[75]

Although they are very similar, "a deferred prosecution agreement is typically predicated upon the filing of a formal charging document by the government, and the agreement is filed with the appropriate court." On the other hand, a non-prosecution agreement does not involve filing of formal charges and "the agreement is maintained by the parties rather than being filed with a court."[76]

In either case, an agreement gives both parties resolution without the expensive ordeal and uncertain outcome of a criminal trial and its attendant appeals. As part of, or in conjunction with an agreement, a corporation may be induced to shed executives,[77] assist in their prosecution,[78] underwrite extensive remedial action,[79] pay substantial fines,[80] acquiesce in the confiscation of property of considerable value,[81] establish a robust compliance process,[82] and accept an oversight monitor for assurance of its continued good behavior.[83]

The guidelines address deferred prosecution and non-prosecution agreements primarily in their plea bargain instructions.[84] As in the case of individuals, the guidelines remind prosecutors to include at least a basic statement of facts.[85] In the case of government contractors, the guidelines prohibit prosecutors from "negotiat[ing] away an agency's right to debar or delist the corporate defendant."[86] They also discourage agreements that shield individual corporate officers, employees, or agents from liability.[87] Internal memoranda guide negotiation of agreements that feature the appointment of outside experts to serve as monitors of a corporation's continued good behavior.[88]

CONSTITUTIONAL RIGHTS

During a criminal investigation and throughout the course of criminal proceedings, corporations and other legal entities enjoy many, but not all, of the constitutional rights implicated in the criminal investigation or prosecution of an individual.

Ex Post Facto

The Constitution's ex post facto clauses condemn retroactive criminal laws, state or federal.[89] In rough terms, the ex post facto clauses prohibit: "1st. Every law that makes an action done before the passing of the law, and which was innocent when done, criminal; and punishes such action.

2d. Every law that aggravates a crime, or makes it greater than it was, when committed. 3d. Every law that changes the punishment, and inflicts a greater punishment, than the law annexed to the crime, when committed. 4th. Every law that alters the legal rules of evidence, and receives less, or different, testimony, than the law required at the time of the commission of the offence, in order to convict the offender."[90]

In cases involving corporate defendants, federal courts have generally proceeded directly to an ex post facto analysis, without pausing to question whether the prohibition applies to such defendants.[91]

First Amendment

The Supreme Court has stated often that corporations are entitled to First Amendment protections.[92] "[I]n the context of political speech, the Government may [not] impose restrictions on certain disfavored speakers" be they individuals or corporations.[93] Nor may corporations suffer content-based blanket proscriptions of their truthful speech when it relates to lawful commercial activity.[94]

Fourth Amendment

The Fourth Amendment condemns unreasonable searches and seizures. Ordinarily, a government search or a seizure is unreasonable unless it is conducted pursuant to a warrant issued on the basis of probable cause.[95] "Corporations can claim no equality with individuals in the enjoyment of a [Fourth Amendment] right to privacy."[96] Nevertheless, it cannot "be claimed that corporations are without some Fourth Amendment rights."[97] At the turn of the 20th century, the Supreme Court acknowledged that corporations enjoyed the protection of the Fourth Amendment when faced with boundless government subpoenas.[98] In later cases, it found the Fourth Amendment's commands had been breached when officers seized a company's records and ledgers, once without a warrant and once with an invalid warrant.[99]

The extent of the Amendment's protection will often turn not upon the nature of the subject to the search entity but the nature of its activities and the government's purpose for the search or seizure. In a regulatory context, commercial activities, corporate or otherwise, may be subject to reasonable warrantless inspections or inquiries bereft of probable cause, under some circumstances.[100] The courts continue to affirm, however, that corporate entities may claim Fourth Amendment protection in cases involving searches and seizures occurring on commercial premises but conducted in the course of a criminal investigation.[101]

Fifth Amendment

Of the rights which the Fifth Amendment guarantees, two have been denied corporations. "[A] corporation has no Fifth Amendment privilege" against self-incrimination,[102] nor does it have a right to grand jury indictment.[103] Of the others, two—Due Process, and Double Jeopardy—either have been said to protect corporations or have been construed to protect corporations.

Due Process

> No person shall be held to answer for a capital, or otherwise infamous crime, unless on a presentment or indictment of a Grand Jury ... ; nor shall any person be subject for the same offence to be twice put in jeopardy of life or limb; nor shall be compelled in any criminal case to be a witness against himself, nor be deprived of life, liberty, or property, without due process of law; nor shall private property be taken for public use, without just compensation. U.S. Const. Amend. V.
>
> . . . [N]or shall any State deprive any person of life, liberty, or property, without due process of law; nor deny to any person within its jurisdiction the equal protection of the laws. U.S. Const. Amend. XIV, §1.

The Fifth Amendment Due Process Clause limits the governmental prerogatives of the federal government; the Fourteenth Amendment Due Process Clause limits the prerogatives of the states. Nevertheless, the Supreme Court has recognized that many of the restrictions of the Bill of Rights, binding on the federal government, are—by virtue of the inclusion of those restrictions within the Fourteenth Amendment's understanding of due process—binding on the states under the same standards.[104]

The Supreme Court has said long and often that a corporation is a "person" for purposes of the Fourteenth Amendment.[105] Moreover, the courts have acknowledged the access of corporations to various due process rights, for example, the right to challenge a court's personal jurisdiction over them[106] or "the right to be heard at a meaningful time and in a meaningful manner before being deprived of a protected interest in liberty or property."[107]

On the other hand, the Supreme Court has said that the states of the United States are not "persons" for Fifth Amendment Due Process Clause purposes.[108] The lower federal courts have followed suit with observations that neither the political subdivisions of the states nor foreign governments are "persons" for purposes of the Due Process Clause.[109]

Double Jeopardy

The circuit courts have concluded that corporations are entitled to protection against double jeopardy.[110] In addition, the Supreme Court has upheld a corporation's double jeopardy challenge without recognizing the right in so many words.[111]

Sixth Amendment

The Sixth Amendment guarantees anyone accused of a federal crime several rights: the right to notice of the charges, to the assistance of counsel, to a public and speedy trial before a jury where the crime occurred, to call witnesses, and to confront his accusers.[112] The text implies the rights are available to anyone, corporate or otherwise, accused of a crime.[113]

Assistance of Counsel

A corporation accused of a crime has the right to the assistance of counsel in its defense.[114] A corporation, however, is not entitled to appointment of counsel at public expense to represent it.[115]

Notice of Charges

The Sixth Amendment assures the accused that he will be "informed of the nature and cause of the accusation."[116] Rule 7(c)(1) of the Federal Rules of Criminal Procedure carries forward the assurance regardless of whether the accused is charged by indictment or information.[117]

Public Trial

In the presence of prejudicial pre-trial publicity or inflamed public sentiment, the right to a public trial may conflict with an accused's Fifth Amendment due process right to a fair trial and his Sixth Amendment right to trial by an impartial jury.[118] Moreover, "the public trial right extends beyond the accused and can be invoked under the First Amendment."[119]

Speedy Trial

The courts use a balancing test to determine whether an accused has been denied his right to a speedy trial. The analysis consists of weighing "the length of [the] delay, the reason for the delay the defendant's assertion of his right, and [the extent] of prejudice to the defendant [caused by the delay]."[120] The courts have used this constitutional analysis when the accused is a corporation.[121] It is in this context, that the corporate right to a public trial is most often asserted.

Jury Trial

The Sixth Amendment assures an accused of the right to a jury in serious criminal cases. In three cases involving legal entities—two labor unions and a corporation—the Supreme Court made it clear that an accused facing a substantial criminal fine has the right to a jury trial.[122]

Venue

By virtue of the Sixth Amendment and Article III, all federal criminal trials must be held in the state and judicial district in which the crime occurs.[123] The venue standards which the courts use for individuals and for corporations are the same.[124]

Call Witnesses and Confrontation

The accused in a criminal proceeding enjoys the rights under the Sixth Amendment "to be confronted with the witnesses against [and] to have compulsory process for obtaining witnesses in his favor."[125] The right to confrontation includes the instruction that "testimonial statements of witnesses absent from trial can be admitted only where the declarant is unavailable, and only where the defendant has had a prior opportunity to cross-examine.[126] Under the right to compulsory process "at a minimum, ... criminal defendants have the right to the government's assistance in compelling the attendance of favorable witnesses at trial and right to put before the jury evidence that might influence the determination of guilt."[127] The rights ensure the integrity of the criminal fact-finding process.[128] The sparse case law suggests they are available to corporations.[129]

Eighth Amendment

The Eighth Amendment states that excessive fines may not be imposed. A fine is excessive if it is grossly disproportionate to gravity of the crime for which the defendant was convicted.[130] A few courts avoid the question by noting that the Supreme Court has never decided whether the Eighth Amendment applies to corporations.[131] Others have ruled against corporations on the merits.[132]

SENTENCING GUIDELINES

Corporations cannot be incarcerated. Nor can they be put to death.[133] Otherwise, corporations and individuals face many of the same consequences following conviction. Corporations can be fined.[134] They can be placed on probation.[135] They can be ordered to pay restitution.[136] Their property can be confiscated.[137] They can be barred from engaging in various types of commercial activity.

Corporations and individuals alike are sentenced in the shadow of the federal Sentencing Guidelines. Federal courts must begin the sentencing process for felonies or class A misdemeanors with a calculation of the sentencing ranges recommended by the Sentencing Guidelines.[138] When they impose sentence, they must consider the recommendation along with the factors prescribed in 18 U.S.C. 3553(a).[139] Appellate courts review the sentences imposed an abuse of discretion standard and will overturn lower court sentences that are procedurally or substantively unreasonable.[140] A sentence is procedurally unreasonable when the sentencing court fails to correctly identify and apply the appropriate Sentencing Guidelines' recommended sentencing range.[141] A sentence is substantively unreasonable when it is unduly harsh or unduly lenient or otherwise inexpedient.[142]

The Sentencing Guidelines for organizations measure punishment according to the seriousness of the offense as well as the defendant's culpability and history of misconduct. On the other hand, they reward self-disclosure, cooperation, restitution, and preventive measures. The Guidelines supply special corporate sentencing directions for fines, probation, forfeiture, special assessments, and remedial sanctions.

Fines

The corporate fine Guidelines begin with the premise that a totally corrupt corporation should be fined out of existence, if the statutory maximum permits.[143] A corporation operated for criminal purposes or by criminal means should be fined at a level sufficient to strip it of all of its assets.[144] On the other hand, a fine need not be imposed at all, if it would render full victim restitution impossible.[145]

Otherwise, corporations face different fine standards depending upon the offense of conviction. In chapter 8C, the Guidelines set specific standards for crimes with a commercial flavor—antitrust, smuggling, and gambling offenses, for instance.[146] The Sentencing Commission explicitly declined to promulgate special corporate fine standards for other offenses.[147] Instead, corporate fines for such offenses are governed by two general statutory sentencing provisions.[148] One, §3571, sets the permissible maximum amount for any fine.[149] The other, §3553, outlines the sentencing factors and procedures applicable to both individuals and corporations.[150] The limited case law suggests that sentencing courts may disregard the Guidelines completely in the case of a corporation convicted of one of these other offenses.[151]

For the offense to which Chapter 8C's fine provisions apply, a sentencing court must begin by deciding whether the defendant entity is able to pay a fine.[152] If so, the amount of an organization's fine is determined by the applicable offense level and the level of its culpability.[153] An organization's offense level is calculated in the same manner as an offense level for an individual but without the adjustments for things like vulnerability of the victim or role in the offense.[154] Unless the amount of gain or loss associated with the offense is greater, the organization's base fine is pegged at one of 33 levels corresponding to its offense level—from $5,000 for an offense level of 6 or less to $72.5 million for an offense level of 38 or more.[155]

The applicable fine range is then ascertained by multiplying the amount assigned to the offense level by minimum and maximum factors determined by the corporation's culpability score.[156] A corporation's score sheet begins at 5.[157] Points are added or subtracted to reflect greater or less culpability.[158] The lowest culpability score merits a range ascertained by multiplying the offense level amount by .05 (setting the bottom of the range) and 0.2 (setting the top).[159] Conversely, the highest culpability score merits a range ascertained by multiplying the offense level amount by 2.0 (setting the bottom of the range) and 4.0 (setting the top).[160]

The Guidelines then identify 11 factors to be considered when deciding where within the applicable range a corporation ought to be fined.[161] The absence of an effective ethics and compliance program is perhaps the most distinctive factor on the list. The Guidelines also identify a number of circumstances that may require or argue for a fine outside of the recommended range. First, the sentence imposed must conform to statutory requirements. Thus, applicable statutory maximums or minimums trump any conflicting Guideline sentencing range boundaries.[162] Second, the sentencing process may leave the corporation with the windfall from its misconduct. Consequently, the Guidelines recommend that the fine level be set so as to disgorge any illegally gotten gains that would otherwise be left to a corporation after the payment of its fine, compliance with the restitution order, or other remedial costs.[163] On the other side, a fine below the recommended range should be imposed when necessary to permit restitution or may be below that range when the corporation will be unable to pay a higher fine even on an installment basis.[164] A below-range corporate fine may also be fitting in light of individual fines imposed upon the owners of a closely held corporation.[165]

The Guidelines supply several examples of when a fine outside the recommended range might be considered. A fine above the range (referred to as upward departures) may be warranted when

- the offense resulted in a risk of death or serious bodily injury;[166]
- the offense constituted a threat to national security;[167]
- the offense presented a threat to the environment;[168]
- the offense presented a threat to the market;[169]
- the offense involved official corruption;[170]
- appropriate to offset reductions attributable to compliance programs;[171] and
- the corporation's culpability score exceeds the limit for additional multipliers.[172]

Departures below the range (referred to as downward departures) may be warranted when

- the corporation provides substantial assistance to authorities;[173]
- the corporation is a public entity, for example, a local governmental agency;[174]
- the corporation's beneficiaries (other than stockholders) are also victims of the offense;[175] and
- the corporation's remedial costs far exceed its gains from the misconduct.[176]

Probation

Corporations convicted of a federal crime must be placed on probation, if the court elects not to fine them.[177] If they are fined, the court may also sentence them to probation.[178] The court impose a probationary term of no more than five years.[179] In the case of felony convictions, the term must be for at least one year.[180]

The Guidelines call for probation as a means of ensuring that convicted corporations comply with their obligations to pay a fine or special assessment, make restitution, establish a compliance program, perform community service, or comply with the court's remedial orders.[181] They also find probation appropriate when

- the organization committed the offense within five years of a prior similar conviction;[182]
- a senior corporate official involved in the offense within five years was involved in a prior similar offense;[183]
- necessary to reduce the risk of future criminal misconduct on the part of the corporation;[184] or
- necessary in order to comply with the sentencing directives of 18 U.S.C.3553(a)(2), i.e., the need to
  - reflect the seriousness of the offense, promote respect for the law, and provide just punishment,
  - afford adequate deterrence,
  - protect the public, and
  - effectively provide for offender training, care, and correctional treatment.[185]

The only mandatory condition of corporate probation is a requirement that the corporation not engage in any further criminal conduct.[186] The array of discretionary probationary conditions under the Guidelines includes requirements that the corporation

- publicize its conviction at its own expense;[187]
- establish and maintain a compliance program;[188]
- notify its employees and shareholders of its offense and compliance program;[189]
- notify or periodically report to the court or the probation service on its finances, compliance program, or involvement in government investigations orproceedings;[190]
- undergo periodic audits at its own expense;[191] or
- make periodic restitution or fine payments.[192]

In addition, a sentencing court remains free to impose any probationary condition that is reasonably necessary and related to the considerations prescribed for sentencing generally under 18 U.S.C. 3553(a), (b)(2).[193]

In response to a corporation's failure to comply with the conditions of its probation, a court may resentence the corporation, extend the term of its probationary period, or impose additional probationary conditions.[194]

Special Assessments

Corporations are subject to a special assessment upon conviction at a rate of $400 for each felony count, $125 for class A misdemeanor count, $50 for each class B misdemeanor count, and $25 for each class C or infraction count.[195]

Restitution, Compliance Programs, and Other Remedial Sentences

Restitution

Depending on the nature of the offense, a court may be required to order a convicted corporation to pay victim restitution. In other instances, it may do so as a matter of discretion. In still others, the court may impose restitution as a condition of probation or pursuant to a plea bargain.[196]

Restitution is required when a defendant has been convicted of

- a crime of violence;[197]
- a crime against property including fraud;[198]
- maintaining a crack house;[199]
- tampering with consumer products;[200]
- theft of medical products;[201]
- sexual abuse;[202]
- child pornography;[203]
- domestic violence;[204]
- telemarketing fraud;[205]
- child support;[206]
- copyright and trademark infringement;[207]
- production of methamphetamines;[208] or
- human trafficking.[209]

The court may order restitution when a corporation is convicted of

- any offense under title 18 of the U.S. Code for which mandatory restitution is notrequired;[210]
- transportation of hazardous materials;[211]
- air transportation of hazardous materials;[212]
- air piracy;[213]
- interference with a flight crew;[214] or
- violations of the Controlled Substances Act under 21 U.S.C. 841 (possession with intent to distribute), 848 (drug kingpin), 849 (trafficking a truck stops or rest stops), 856 (maintaining a crack house), 861 (using children in drug operations), 863 (drug paraphernalia).[215]

In the absence of other specific authority, the court may order restitution as a condition of probation[216] or pursuant to a plea bargain.[217] In related matter, corporate defendants convicted of fraud may be ordered to pay for victim notification.[218]

Compliance Programs

The Guidelines' effective compliance and ethics program features are perhaps its most well-known corporate component. A corporation that lacks such a program is likely to have one imposed at sentencing or pursuant to a plea bargain. As noted earlier, a corporation that has one is likely to fare better during the investigation, bargaining, and sentencing phases of a criminal case.

The Guidelines envision programs that promote an ethical and law-abiding culture within a corporation and that are calculated to identify and prevent criminal misconduct within the corporation.[219] The elements of such a program consist of the following:

1. An established set of standards and procedures designed to detect and prevent criminal misconduct.[220]
2. Senior management involvement in the program including its day to day operations.[221]
3. Minimizing the operation participation of those previously ethically challenged.[222]
4. Training corporate employees and agents.[223]
5. Monitoring, auditing, and evaluating the program.[224]

6. Encourage and reward performance consistent with the program's goals; discipline inconsistent conduct.[225]
7. Responding appropriately to the discovery of in-house criminal conduct.[226]

Community Service

The Guidelines provide that a corporation may be sentenced to perform community service related to the harm caused by its offense as a probationary condition as long as the corporation has skills, facilities, or knowledge particularly suited to task.[227] Otherwise, it suggests that fines or other monetary sanctions may be more appropriate and that service unrelated to harm caused by the offense is not consistent with the Guideline.[228]

Other Remedial Orders

The court may impose other probationary conditions that address the harm caused or to be caused by the corporation's crime, including in cases of substantial anticipated future harm the creation of a trust fund.[229]

Forfeiture

Forfeiture, the confiscation of property as a consequence of its relation to a criminal offense, is a creature of statute.[230] Some forfeiture statutes are remedial, some punitive, and some serve purposes.[231] The Guidelines confirm that the property of a corporation is no less subject to confiscation than the property of an individual.[232]

End Notes

[1] *United States v. Agosto-Vega*, 617 F.3d 541, 552-53 (1st Cir. 2010); *United States v. Philip Morris USA, Inc.*, 566 F.3d 1095, 1118-119 (D.C.Cir. 2009); *United States v. Singh*, 518 F.3d 236, 249 (4th Cir. 2008); *accord, United States v. Jorgensen*, 144 F.3d 550, 560 (8th Cir. 1998); *United States v. Investment Enterprises, Inc.*, 10 F.3d 263, 266 (5th Cir. 1994); *United States v. Twentieth Century Fox Film Corp.*, 882 F.2d 656, 660 (2d Cir. 1989); *United States v. Gold*, 743 F.2d 800, 822-23 (11th Cir. 1984); *United States v. Beusch*, 596 F.2d 871, 877-78 (9th Cir. 1979); *United States v. Carter*, 311 F.2d 934, 941-42 (6th Cir. 1963).

[2] 1 BLACKSTONE, COMMENTARIES ON THE LAWS OF ENGLAND 464 (1765) (transliteration provided).

[3] WHARTON, TREATISE ON THE CRIMINAL LAW OF THE UNITED STATES 58 (2d ed. 1852)("[A] corporation may be indicted for a breach of duty imposed on it by law ... Whether this criminal liability extends to acts of misfeasance is more doubtful").

[4] 1 BISHOP, COMMENTARIES ON THE CRIMINAL LAW §420 (7th ed. 1882)("But while the courts everywhere hold corporations to be thus indictable for non-feasance, it is by some denied that they are for misfeasance.... But the contrary is established in England ... This English doctrine ... is the better doctrine in principle").

[5] *New York Central & Hudson River Railroad Co. v. United States*, 212 U.S. 481, 494-95 (1909).

[6] Brickley, *Corporate Criminal Accountability: A Brief History and an Observation*, 60 WASHINGTON UNIVERSITY LAW QUARTERLY 393, 411 (1982), quoting, *State v. First National Bank*, 2 S.D. 568, 571, 51 N.W. 587, 587 (1892); see also, PERKINS, CRIMINAL LAW 640-41 (2d ed. 1969)("If a corporation had such a duty which it neglected to perform no sound reason against its conviction was available, and it was but a short step from recognition of corporate guilt for a civil offense based upon nonfeasance to such guilt based upon affirmative misconduct. Since such an offense does not have the normal mens-rea requirement for criminal guilty, and conviction may be supported on the basis *of respondeat superior*, the possibility of convicting a corporation of a civil offense became firmly established. For years it seemed the change from the original position would stop at this point and that a corporation would be held incapable of committing a true crime on the ground that it could not have means rea.... Gradually, however, the change moved over into the area of true crime").

[7] *Clinton v. City of New York*, 524 U.S. 417, 428 n.13 (1998).

[8] 1 U.S.C. 1.

[9] E.g., *United States v. A & P Trucking Co.*, 358 U.S. 121, 123 (1958)(violation of Interstate Commerce Commission safety regulations, former 18 U.S.C. 835 (1958 ed.)); *United States v. Polizzi*, 500 F.2d 856, 907 (9th Cir. 1974) (violation of the Travel Act, 18 U.S.C. 1952); *Western Laundry and Linen Rental Co. v. United States*, 424 F.2d 441, 443 (9th Cir. 1970)(antitrust violations under the Sherman Act, 15 U.S.C. 1); *United States v. Hougland Barge Line, Inc.*, 387 F.Supp. 1110, 1114 (W.D.Pa. 1974) (conspiracy, 18 U.S.C. 371).

[10] 18 U.S.C. 1961(3).

[11] 26 U.S.C. 7701(a)(1)-(3).

[12] E.g., 42 U.S.C. 6903(15) for purposes of the Resource Conservation and Recovery Act (RCRA), "the term 'person' means an individual, trust, firm, joint stock company, corporation (including a government corporation), partnership, association, State, municipality, commission, political subdivision of a State, or any interstate body and shall include each department, agency, and instrumentality of the United States."

[13] *Newport v. Fast Concerts, Inc.*, 453 U.S. 247, 258-71 (1981)(municipalities are immune from punitive damages under 42 U.S.C. 1983, for civil rights violations); *Gentry v. Resolution Trust Corp.*, 937 F.2d 899, 914 (3d Cir. 1991)("the prevailing punitive nature of section 1964(c)'s compulsory award of treble damages convinces us that Congress, in keeping with the common law, did not intend to subject municipal corporations to RICO liability").

[14] *United States v. Singh*, 518 F.3d 236, 249-50 (4th Cir. 2008)("a corporation accused is liable for the criminal acts of its employees and agents acting within the scope of their employment for the benefit of the corporation and such liability arises if the employee or agent acted for his own benefit as well as that of his employer"); *United States v. Potter*, 463 F.3d 9, 25 (1st Cir. 2006); *United States v. Jorgensen*, 144 F.3d 550, 560 (8th Cir. 1998); *United States v. Sun Diamond Growers*, 138 F.3d 961 (D.C.Cir. 1998).

[15] *United States v. Agosto-Vega*, 617 F.3d 541, 25 (1st Cir. 2010) ("[t]he test is whether the agent is performing acts of the kind which he is authorized to perform and those acts are motivated—at least in part—by an intent to benefit the corporation"); *United States v. Singh*, 518 F.3d at 250-51; *United States v. Gold*, 743 F.2d 800, 823 (11th Cir. 1984)("the servant's conduct is within the scope of his employment if it is of the kind he is employed to

perform, occurs substantially within the authorized limits of time and space, and is actuated, at least in part by a purpose to serve the master").

[16] *United States v. Potter*, 463 F.3d 9, 26 (1st Cir. 2006); *United States v. Automated Medical Laboratories*, 770 F.2d 399, 406 (4th Cir. 1985); *United States v. Ionia Management S.A.*, 525 F.Supp.2d 319, 324 (D. Conn. 2007).

[17] MODEL PENAL CODE §2.07 (1985)("A corporation may be convicted of the commission of an offense if (a) the offense is a violation ... in which a legislative purpose to impose liability on corporations plainly appears ... or (b) the offense consists of an omission to discharge a specific duty or affirmative performance imposed on corporations by law; or (c) the commission of the offense was authorized, requested, commanded, performed or recklessly tolerated by the board of directors or by a high managerial agent acting in behalf of the corporation within the scope of his office or employment. (2) When absolute liability is imposed for the commission of an offense, a legislative purpose to impose liability on a corporation shall be assumed, unless the contrary plainly appears ... (5) In any prosecution of a corporation ... for the commission of an offense included within the terms of Subsection (1)(a) ... it shall be a defense ... that the high managerial agent having supervisory responsibility over the subject matter of the offense employed due diligence to prevent it commission ... ").

[18] E.g., ARIZ. REV. STAT. ANN. §13-305 ("A. Notwithstanding any other provisions of law, an enterprise commits an offense if: 1. The conduct constituting the offense consists of a failure to discharge a specific duty imposed by law; or 2. The conduct undertaken in behalf of the enterprise and constituting the offense, is engaged in, authorized, solicited, commanded or recklessly tolerated by the directors of the enterprise in any manner or by a high managerial agent acting within the scope of employment; or 3. The conduct constituting the offense is engaged in by an agent of the enterprise while acting within the scope of employment and in behalf of the enterprise; and (a) the offense is a misdemeanor or petty offense; or (b) The offense is defined by a statute which imposed criminal liability on an enterprise").

[19] *United States v. Philip Morris USA, Inc.*, 566 F.3d 1095, 1118 (D.C.Cir. 2009), citing, *N.Y. Central & Hudson River R.R. Co. v. United States*, 212 U.S. 481, 495 (1909), and *United States v. A & P Trucking Co.*, 358 U.S. 121, 125 (1958); see also, *United States v. LaGrou Distribution Systems*, 466 F.3d 585, 591 (7th Cir. 2006).

[20] *United States v. LaGrou Distribution Systems, 466 F.3d at 591; United States v. Route, 2 Box 472, 136 Acres More or Less (Dyer's Trout Farms, Inc.)*, 60 F.3d 1523, 1527 (11th Cir. 1995*); United States v. Bank of New England*, 821 F.2d 844, 855 (1st Cir. 1987).

[21] Compare, *United States v. Bank of New England*, 821 F.2d at 856 (internal citations omitted)("A collective knowledge instruction is entirely appropriate in the context of corporate criminal liability. The acts of a corporation are, after all, simply the acts of all of its employees operating within the scope of their employment. The law on corporate criminal liability reflects this. Similarly, the knowledge obtained by corporate employees acting within the scope of their employment is imputed to the corporation. Corporations compartmentalize knowledge, subdividing the elements of specific duties and operations into smaller components. The aggregate of those components constitutes the corporation's knowledge of a particular operation. It is irrelevant whether employees administering one component of an operation know the specific activities of employees administering another aspect of the operation: A corporation cannot plead innocence by asserting that the information obtained by several employees was not acquired by any one individual who then would have comprehended its full import. Rather the corporation is considered to have acquired the collective knowledge of its employees and is held responsible for their failure to act accordingly"), with, *United States v. Philip Morris USA, Inc.*, 566 F.3d at 1122 ("Like Defendants and other courts, we are dubious of the legal soundness of the "collective intent" theory. *Saba [v. Compagnie Nationale Air France*, 78 F.3d 664, 670 n.6 (D.C. Cir. 1996)('corporate knowledge of certain facts [can be] accumulated from the knowledge of

various individuals, but the proscribed intent (willfulness) depends[s] on the wrongful intent of specific employees')" and *Southland Securities v. Inspire Insurance Solutions*, 365 F.3d 353, 366 (5th Cir. 2004)("For purposes of determining whether a statement made by the corporation was made by it with the requisite Rule 10(b) scienter we believe it appropriate to look to the state of mind of the individual corporate official or officials who make or issue the statement (or order or approve it or its making or issuance, or who furnish information or language for inclusion therein, or the like) rather than generally to the collective knowledge of all the corporation's officers and employees acquired in the course of their employment").

[22] *United States v. Wise*, 370 U.S. 405, 407 (1962).

[23] *Id.* at 409, citing, *United States v. Dotterweich*, 320 U.S. 277 (1943).

[24] 18 U.S.C. 371.

[25] *United States v. Sain*, 141 F.3d 463, 475 (3d Cir. 1998); *United States v. Hughes Aircraft Co.*, 20 F.3d 974, 979 (9th Cir. 1994); *United States v. Ames Sintering Co.*, 927 F.2d 236-37 (6th Cir. 1990); *United States v. Hugh Chalmers Chevrolet-Toyota, Inc.*, 800 F.2d 737, 738 (8th Cir. 1986).

[26] *United States v. Stevens*, 909 F.2d 431, 432-34 (11th Cir. 1990); *United States v. Peters*, 732 F.2d 1004, 1008 n.6 (1st Cir. 1984).

[27] *Pinkerton v. United States*, 328 U.S. 640, 647-48 (1946); *United States v. Singh*, 518 F.3d 236, 252-53 (4th Cir. 2008); *United States v. Skilling*, 554 F.3d 529, 547 (5th Cir. 2009), aff'd in part and vac'd in part on other grounds, 130 S.Ct. 2896 (2010); *United States v. Sklena*, 692 F.3d 725, 729-30 (7th Cir. 2012); *United States v. Clark*, 717 F.3d 790, 808-809 (10th Cir. 2013).

[28] 18 U.S.C. 2(a); see e.g., *United States v. Sain*, 141 F.3d 463, (3d Cir. 1998)("an individual who causes a corporation to commit a crime is criminally liable for the corporations' criminal conduct as an aider and abettor ... "); *United States v. Cohen*, 260 F.3d 68, 77-8 (2d Cir. 2001)(the president of a company which operated an off-shore internet gambling site was in a position to cause the company's continued violation of the Wire Act (18 U.S.C. 1084)).

[29] *Nye & Nissen v. United States*, 336 U.S. 613, 619 (1949); see also, *United States v. Davis*, 717 F.3d 28, 33 (1st Cir. 2013)("Aiding and abetting requires proof that: 1) the substantive offense was actually committed; 2) the defendant assisted in the commission of that crime or caused it to be committed; and 3) the defendant intended to assist in the commission of that crime and or to cause it to be committed. Moreover ... a culpable aider and abetter need not perform the substantive offense, be present when it is performed, or be aware of the details of its execution"); *United States v. Joseph*, 709 F.3d 1082, 1102 (11th Cir. 2013).

[30] *United States v. Rodriguez-Lozada*, 558 F.3d 29, 41 (1st Cir. 2009); *United States v. Dearing*, 504 F.3d 897, 901 (9th Cir. 2007); *United States v. Kemp*, 500 F.3d 257, 293 (3d Cir. 2007).

[31] *United States v. Sain*, 141 F.3d 463, 474-75 (3d Cir. 1998)("AEC, because it is a corporation, is a separate legal entity, even though Sain owned all the stock. Thus, it has the capacity of being aided and abetted. To hold otherwise would allow the controlling stockholder of a corporation to enjoy the benefits of the corporate form, protection from personal liability for corporation's debts, without accepting the burden of assuming criminal responsibility when the individual causes the corporation to commit a crime.... Even assuming that Sain is correct that it was impossible for him to conspire with AEC, that conclusion does not preclude imposition of aiding and abetting responsibility. Arguably, Sain could not conspire with AEC because AEC could not form the mental state required to conspire with another. This is because a corporation is a conspirator only pursuant to respondeat superior liability. If an agent of the corporation conspires with another individual, the corporation for which the individual is the agent may be criminally liable. However, there must be at least two natural individuals for a conspiracy involving a corporation to exist because two entities must have the required mental state to form a conspiracy. The aiding and abetting statute allows for broader liability and does not require proof that an unwitting entity being used to commit the crime possessed any mental state. 18 U.S.C. §2(b) ('Whoever willfully causes

an act to be done which if directly performed by him or another would be an offense against the United States, is punishable as a principal.'). Only the person causing the unwitting entity to act must possess the knowing mental state. Therefore, an individual who causes a corporation to commit a crime is criminally liable for the corporation's criminal conduct as an aider and abettor even if the corporation does not act with a knowing mental state.. For that reason, conviction of Sain was proper even assuming arguendo that Sain caused AEC to unwittingly commit the crime. Thus, the district court committed no error in sustaining Sain's conviction as an aider and abettor").

[32] 18 U.S.C. 3, 4.

[33] *United States v. White Eagle*, 721 F.3d 1108, 1119 (9th Cir. 2013)("Misprision of a felony in violation of 18 U.S.C. §4 requires the government to establish: (1) the commission and completion of a felony by a third party, (2) the defendant's knowledge of the felony, 3) the defendant's failure to notify the authorities, and (4) that the defendant took an affirmative step to conceal the crime"); *United States v. Boyd*, 640 F.3d 657, 662 (6th Cir. 2011); *United States v. Gebbie*, 294 F.3d 540, 544 (3d Cir. 2002); *United States v. Cefalu*, 85 F.3d 964, 868 (2d Cir. 1996).

[34] *United States v. Boyd*, 640 F.3d at 662; *United States v. Gerrhard*, 615 F.3d 7, 23-4 (1st Cir. 2010); *United States v. Gianakos*, 415 F.3d 912, 919 n.4 (8th Cir. 2005); *United States v. DeLaRose*, 171 F.3d 215, 221 (5th Cir. 1999); *United States v. Osborn*, 120 F.3d 59, 63 (7th Cir. 1997).

[35] E.g., 18 U.S.C. 1001 (false material statements relating to a matter with the jurisdiction of a federal department or agency), 1512 (witness tampering or destruction of evidence), 1520 (destruction of federal audit records).

[36] *United States v. Dotterweich*, 320 U.S. 277 (1943); *United States v. Park*, 421 U.S. 658 (1975).

[37] *United States v. Park*, 421 U.S. at 669, quoting, *United States v. Dotterweich*, 320 U.S. at 280-81.

[38] *Staples v. United States*, 511 U.S. 600, 607 (1994).

[39] *Id.*

[40] *Id.*, quoting, *United States v. Balint*, 258 U.S. 250, 254 (1922).

[41] *Staples v. United States*, 511 U.S. at 607. See e.g., *United States v. Jorgensen*, 144 F.3d 550, 560 (8th Cir. 1998)(internal citations omitted)("A corporate officer who is in a 'responsible relationship' to an activity within a company that violates provisions of the federal food laws, such as meat misbranding, can be held criminally responsible even though that officer did not personally engage in that activity. As previously noted, the misbranding provisions of which the corporate officers were convicted required the officer to act with an intent to defraud. Thus, the jury could convict a defendant corporate officer if it found a defendant: (1) had an intent to defraud; and (2) either personally participated in the misbranding or was in a responsible relationship within the company regarding the misbranding of meat").

[42] *United States v. Park*, 421 U.S. at 673-74.

[43] *Wayte v. United States*, 470 U.S. 598, 607 (1985)(internal citations and quotation marks omitted)("In our criminal justice system, the Government retains broad discretion as to whom to prosecute. So long as the prosecutor has probable cause to believe that the accused committed an offense defined by statute, the decision whether or not to prosecute, and what charge to file or bring before a grand jury, generally rests entirely in his discretion"); *United States v. Nixon*, 418 U.S. 683, 693 (1974)("[T]he Executive Branch has exclusive authority and absolute discretion to decide whether to prosecute a case"). *United States v. Armstrong*, 517 U.S. 456, 464 (1996)("The Attorney General and United States Attorneys retain broad discretion to enforce the Nation's criminal laws. They have this latitude because they are designated by statute as the President's delegates to help him discharge his constitutional responsibility to take Care that the Laws be Faithfully executed"), citing inter alia, U.S. Const. Art. II, §3, and 28 U.S.C. 516, 547.

[44] *Wayte v. United States*, 470 U.S. at 608 (internal citations and quotation marks omitted) ("[A]lthough prosecutorial discretion is broad, it is not unfettered ... In particular, the

decision to prosecute may not be deliberately based upon an unjustifiable standard such as race, religion, or other arbitrary classification including the exercise of protected statutory and constitutional rights"); *United States v. Armstrong*, 517 U.S. at 464 ("Of course, a prosecutor's discretion is subject to constitutional constraints").

[45] *U.S. Attorneys' Manual (USAM)*, §§9-27.000 et seq., and §§9-28.000 et seq., respectively, available at http://www.justice.gov/usao/eousa/foia_reading_room/usam/title9. Although they refer to "business organizations" and "corporations," the business organization principles construe those terms broadly, *USAM* §9-28.000 n.1 ("While these guidelines refer to corporations, they apply to the consideration of the prosecution of all types of business organizations, including partnerships, sole proprietorships, government entities, and unincorporated associations")

[46] *USAM*, §9-27.200[B]. Grounds for suspicion, short of probable cause, may justify further investigation, *id.*

[47] *USAM*, §9-27.220[A].

[48] *Id.*

[49] *USAM* §9-28.500.

[50] *USAM* §9-28.600.

[51] *USAM* §9-28.800.

[52] *USAM* §9-28.720, 9-28.750.

[53] *USAM* §§9-28.700, 9-28.710, 9-28.740, 9-28.760.

[54] *USAM* §9-28.730.

[55] *USAM* §9-28.1000.

[56] *USAM* §9-28.900.

[57] *USAM* §9-28.500[A].

[58] *Id.*

[59] *USAM* §9-28.600[B]("Criminal prosecution of a corporation may be particularly appropriate where the corporation previously had been subject to non-criminal guidance, warnings, or sanctions, or previous criminal charges, and it either had not taken adequate action to prevent future unlawful conduct or had continued to engage in the misconduct in spite of the warnings or enforcement actions taken against it").

[60] *Id.*

[61] *United States v. Potter*, 463 F.3d 9, 26 (1st Cir. 2006); *United States v. Automated Medical Laboratories*, 770 F.2d 399, 406 (4th Cir. 1985); *United States v. Ionia Management S.A.*, 525 F.Supp.2d 319, 324 (D. Conn. 2007).

[62] *USAM* §9-28.800[A]; U.S.S.G. §§8C2.5(f), 8B2.1.

[63] *USAM* §9-28.800[B]("[A] truly effective compliance program ... may result in a decision to charge only the corporation's employees and agents or to mitigate charges or sanctions against the corporation"). An effective compliance program will reduce a convicted corporation's "culpability score" under the Sentencing Guidelines and consequently lower the corporation's ultimate sentencing range, U.S.S.G. §§8C2.5(f), 8A1.2.

[64] *USAM* §9-28.750.

[65] *USAM* §9-28.740 (emphasis added)("A corporation should not be able to escape liability *merely* by offering up its directors, officers, employees, or agents").

[66] See e.g., The McNulty Memorandum's Effect on the Right to Counsel in Corporate Investigations: Hearing Before the Subcomm. on Crime, Terrorism, and Homeland Security of the House Comm. on the Judiciary, 110th Cong., 1st Sess. (2007); Examining Approaches to Corporate Fraud Prosecutions and the Attorney-Client Privilege Under the McNulty Memorandum: Hearing Before the Senate Comm. on the Judiciary, 110th Cong., 1st Sess. (2007); CRS Report RL33842, Prosecutorial Discretion in the Context of Corporate Attorney-Client Relations.

[67] *USAM* §9-28.710; see also, *USAM* §9-28.720 ("Eligibility for cooperation credit is not predicated upon the waiver of attorney-client privilege or work product protection. Instead, the sort of cooperation that is most valuable to resolving allegations of misconduct by a

corporation and its officers, directors, employees, or agents is disclosure of the relevant facts concerning such misconduct").

[68] *USAM* §9-28.730.

[69] *USAM* §9-28.760.

[70] *USAM* §9-28.900.

[71] *USAM* §9-28.1000.

[72] *USAM* §9-27.240.

[73] *USAM* §9-27.1100[B]. Prosecutors will sometimes agree to a combination of criminal and civil sanctions, see e.g., *Johnson & Johnson Agrees to Pay 24.1 Million Criminal Penalty to Remedy Foreign Corrupt Practices Act and Oil for Food Investments*, Department of Justice Press Release (April 8, 2011)(announcing corporate agreement to pay criminal fine of $21.4 million and a Securities Exchange Commission disgorgement penalty of $48.6 million).

[74] Markoff, *Arthur Andersen and the Myth of the Corporate Death Penalty: Corporate Criminal Convictions in the Twenty-First Century*, 15 UNIVERSITY OF PENNSYLVANIA JOURNAL OF BUSINESS LAW 797, 800 (2013)("For many commentators, it is now unquestioned dogma that a criminal indictment alone can easily destroy even a large, powerful corporation").

[75] See generally, Accountability, Transparency, and Uniformity in Corporate Deferred and Non-Prosecution Agreements: Hearing Before the Subcomm. on Commercial and Administrative Law of the House Comm. on the Judiciary, 111th Cong., 1st Sess. (2009); Government Accountability Office, Corporate Crime: Preliminary Observations on DOJ's Use and Oversight of Deferred Prosecution and Non-Prosecution Agreements, GAO-09-636T (2009); Warin, 2013 Mid-Year Update on Corporate Deferred Prosecution and Non-Prosecution Agreements, Harvard Law School Forum on Corporate Governance and Financial Regulation, available at http://blogs.law.harvard.edu/ corpgov/2013/07/24/2013-mid-year-update-on-corporate-deferred-prosecution-and-non-prosecution-agreements.

[76] *Criminal Resource Manual (CRM)* §163 n.2 (Mar. 7, 2008). The distinction is not insignificant, because the courts serve as an additional guarantor of the public interest when they are involved, see e.g., *United States v. Orthofix, Inc.*, ___ F.Supp.2d ___ (2013 WL 3835233)(July 26, 2013 D.Mass.)(rejecting a deferred prosecution agreement as insufficient to protect the public interest).

[77] See e.g., *United States v. Stein*, 541 F.3d 130, 137 (2d Cir. 2008)(internal citations omitted)("KPMG retained Robert S. Bennett ... to formulate a cooperative approach for KPMG to use in dealing with federal authorities 's counsel. Bennett's strategy included a decision to clean house—a determination to ask Jeffrey Stein, Richard Smith, and Jeffrey Eischeid, all senior KPMG partners ... —to leave their positions as deputy chair and chief operating officer of the firm, vice chair-tax services, and a partner in personal financial planning, respectively"). The government subsequently announced a deferred prosecution agreement in which it noted that six former KPMG partners and a former deputy chairman were to be prosecuted, *KPMG to Pay $456 Million for Criminal Violations in Relation to Largest-Ever Tax Shelter Fraud Case*, Department of Justice Press Release (Aug. 29, 2005). Corporate agreements may coincide with individual plea agreements with corporate executives or former executives, see e.g., *Internet Gambling Company PartyGaming PLC Enters Non-Prosecution Agreement with U.S. and Will Forfeit $105 Million*, U.S. Attorney for the Southern District of New York Press Release (April 7, 2009)(noting that PartyGaming's founder and former executive had agreed to forfeit $300 million and plead guilty to gambling charge carrying a maximum term of imprisonment of two years).

[78] See e.g., *UBS AG Non-Prosecution Agreement* ("UBS shall ... (b) truthfully and completely disclose non-privileged information with respect to the activities of UBS, its officers and employees, and other concerning all matters about which the Fraud Section inquires of it ... (c) bring to the Fraud Section's attention all potentially criminal conduct by UBS or any of its employees that relates to violations of U.S. laws (i) concerning fraud or (ii) governing

securities and commodities markets.... "), available at http://www.justice.gov/iso/opa/resources/1392012121911745845757.pdf.

[79] See e.g., *United States v. BP America Inc. (Deferred Prosecution Agreement)* (No. 07-cr-683)(N.D.Ill. Oct.27, 2007)(agreeing to establish a $53,503 million victim restitution fund), available at http://www.justice.gov/criminal/vns/docs/2007/oct/10-25-07bpamerica-dpa.pdf.

[80] See e.g., *United States v. The Royal Bank of Scotland plc (3:13-CR-74-MPS)/United States v. RBS Securities Japan Limited (3:13-CR-73-MPS)*, Department of Justice Press Release (Feb. 13, 2013)(announcing an agreement under which Royal Bank of Scotland and RBS Securities Japan agreed to pay $612 million in criminal penalties).

[81] See e.g., *United States v. Credit Suisse AG (Deferred Prosecution Agreement)*(D.D.C. Dec. 16, 2009)(agreeing to a forfeiture settlement of $268 million), available at http://www.justice.gov/criminal/pr/documents/12-16-09-deferred-%20proseuction-%20agreement.pfd.

[82] See e.g., *United States v. Sigue Corp. (Deferred Prosecution Agreement)*(No. 4:08-cr-00054-RWS) (E.D.Mo. Jan. 28, 2008) (in which Sigue agreed to develop and implement a compliance program which it estimated would cost it $9.7 million), available at http://www.justice.gov/opa/documents/sigue-deferred-prosecution-agreement.pdf.

[83] See e.g., *HSBC Deferred Prosecution Agreement, Attachment B, Corporate Compliance Monitor*, available at http://www.justice.gov/opa/documents/hsbc/dpa-attachment-b.pdf. See also, *United States v. HSBC Bank USA, NA* (2013WL3306161) (No. 12-cr-00763-JG)(E.D.N.Y. July 1, 2013).

[84] *USAM* §9-28.1300; see also, *USAM* §9-27.300 et seq.

[85] *USAM* §9-28.1300[B].

[86] *Id.*

[87] *Id.*

[88] *CRM* §§163 ("Morford Memorandum"), 166 ("Grindler Memorandum"). The recommendations cover selection of a monitor, the monitor's independence, his or her responsibility to oversee compliance with the agreement, development and weight of the monitor's recommendations, reporting newly discovered corporate misconduct, the monitor's tenure, and resolution of disputes between the monitor and the corporation.

[89] U.S. Const. Art. I, §9, cl.3; Art. I, § 10. cl.1.

[90] *Peugh v. United States*, 133 S.Ct. 2072, 2081 (2013), quoting, *Calder v. Bull*, 3 Dall. (U.S.) 386, 390 (1789).

[91] E.g., *Louis Vuitton S.A. v. Spencer Handbags Corp.*, 765 F.2d 966, 971-72 (2d Cir. 1985)(construing amendments to the Trademark Counterfeiting Act narrowly after noting the possibility of an ex post facto violation otherwise); *United States ex rel. Baker v. Community Health Systems*, 709 F.Supp.2d 1084, 1108-112 (D.N.Mex. 2010)(holding that retroactive application of False Claims Act amendments would constitute an ex post facto violation); *United States ex rel. Sanders v. Allison Engine Co., Inc.*, 667 F.Supp.2d 747, 752-58 (S.D.Ohio 2009)(same).

[92] *Citizens United v. Federal Election Comm'n*, 130 S.Ct. 876, 899-900 (2010)(citing two dozen cases for the proposition); see also, *Austin v. Michigan Chamber of Commerce*, 494 U.S. 652, 657 (1990)("The mere fact that the Chamber is a corporation does not remove its speech from the ambit of the First Amendment"); *First National Bank of Boston v. Belliotti*, 435 U.S. 765, 779 n.14 (1978)("In cases where corporate speech has been denied the shelter of the First Amendment, there is no suggestion that the reason was because a corporation rather than an individual or association was involved").

[93] *Citizens United v. Federal Election Comm'n*, 130 S.Ct. at 899.

[94] *Linmark Associates, Inc. v. Willingboro*, 431 U.S. 85, 98 (1977).

[95] "The right of the people to be secure in their persons, houses, papers, and effects, against unreasonable searches and seizures, shall not be violated; and no Warrants shall issue but upon probable cause, supported by Oath or affirmation, and particularly describing the place to be searched, and the persons or things to be seized," U.S. Const. Amend. IV.

[96] *United States v. Morton Salt Co.*, 338 U.S. 632, 652 (1950).

[97] *G.M. Leasing Corp. v. United States*, 429 U.S. 338, 353 (1977).

[98] *Hale v. Henkel,* 201 U.S. 43, 76 (1905)("[W]e do not wish to be understood as holding that a corporation is not entitled to immunity, under the Fourth Amendment, against *unreasonable* searches and seizures. ... We are also of opinion that an order for the production of books and papers may constitute an unreasonable search and seizure within the Fourth Amendment. While a search ordinarily implies a quest by an officer of the law, and a seizure contemplates a forcible dispossession of the owner, still, ... the substance of the offense is the compulsory production of private papers, whether under a search warrant or a *subpoena duces tecum,* against which the person, be he individual or corporation, is entitled to protection. Applying the test of reasonableness to the present case, we think the *subpoena duces tecum* is far too sweeping in its terms to be regarded as reasonable").

[99] *Silverthorne Lumber Co., Inc. v. United States*, 251 U.S. 385 (1920); *Go-Bart Co. v. United States*, 282 U.S. 344 (1931).

[100] *New York v. Burger*, 482 U.S. 691, 702-703 (1987)("Because the owner or operator of commercial premises in a 'closely regulated' industry has a reduced expectation of privacy, the warrant and probable-cause requirements, which fulfill the traditional Fourth Amendment standard of reasonableness for a government search have lessened application in this context.... This warrantless inspection ... will be deemed to be reasonable only so long as three criteria are met. First, there must be a 'substantial' government interest that informs the regulatory scheme pursuant to which the inspection is made.... Second, the warrantless inspections must be 'necessary to further [the] regulatory scheme.... Finally ... the regulatory statute must perform the two functions of a warrant: it must advise the owner of the commercial premises that the search is being made pursuant to the law and has a properly defined scope, and it must limit the discretion of the inspecting officers").

[101] *Club Retro LLC v. Hilton*, 568 F.3d 181, 195 (5th Cir. 2009)("[T]he entry and search of Club Retro violated Club Retro, L.L.C.'s Fourth Amendment right to operate its commercial property free from unreasonable searches and seizures"); *United States v. SDI Future Health Inc.*, 568 F.3d 684, 694 & n.3 (9th Cir. 2009)("The government first argues that Kaplan and Brunk lack standing to challenge the search and seizure of materials from SDI's premises. Wisely, the government does not argue that SDI itself lacks standing to challenge the underlying search and seizure. See *United States v. Leary*, 846 F.2d 592, 596 (10th Cir. 1988)('A corporate defendant has standing with respect to searches of corporate premises and seizure of corporate records')"); *Doe v. Heck*, 327 F.3d 492, 509 n.14 (7th Cir. 2003)("A private school, like any other corporation or business, is entitled to bring a Fourth Amendment challenge for the illegal search of its premises").

[102] *Braswell v. United States*, 487 U.S. 99, 105 (1988); *Louis Vuitton Malletier S.A., v. LY USA, Inc.*, 676 F.3d 83, 92 n.5 (2d Cir. 2012); *Eagle Hospital Physicians, LLC v. SRG Consulting, Inc.*, 561 F.3d 1298, 1303 n.2 (11th Cir. 2009); *Amato v. United States*, 450 F.3d 46, 48 n.2 (1st Cir. 2006)("The collective-entity doctrine recognizes that the Fifth Amendment treats corporations and collective entities differently from individuals. Because corporations and collective entities have no Fifth Amendment privilege against self-incrimination ... the custodian cannot claim a personal Fifth Amendment privilege against the production of corporate records").

[103] *United States v. Macklin*, 389 F.Supp. 272, 273 (S.D.N.Y. 1975), aff'd, 523 F.2d 193 (2d Cir. 1975)("The corporate defendants, unlike defendant Macklin, are not subject to any term of imprisonment if convicted of the charges against them. Accordingly, the charges against them are not 'infamous' within the meaning of the fifth amendment"); see also, *United States v. Yellow Freight System, Inc.*, 637 F.3d 1248, 1253-254 (9th Cir. 1981)(emphasis added and internal citations omitted) ("Relying on United States Supreme Court pronouncements that infamous crimes are those 'punishable by imprisonment in a penitentiary,' defendants contend that they have been charged with infamous crimes and may not be prosecuted except on grand jury indictment. In response, the United States notes that both defendants are corporations and therefore not amenable to imprisonment. It

accordingly contends that this prosecution may proceed by information alone.... Since we hold that imposition of potential imprisonment on individuals violating a criminal statute does not of itself make corporate violations of the same statute infamous crimes, the only remaining question is whether another factor renders the crimes charged in this case infamous ... The class of inherently infamous crimes, *if it exists at all*, would encompass only the most serious mala in se. Regulatory crimes such as those charged in this case, are not inherently infamous"). Note that , Rule 7(a) of the Federal Rules of Criminal Procedure declares, without reference to the class of defendants, that "An offense (other than criminal contempt) must be prosecuted by an indictment if it is punishable (A) death; or (B) by imprisonment for more than one year," unless waived under Rule 7(b).

[104] *Malloy v. Hogan*, 378 U.S. 1, 4-5, 10 (1964)(internal citations omitted)("[S]ome of the personal rights safeguarded by the first eight Amendments against National action may also be safeguarded against state action, because a denial of them would be a denial of due process of law.... We have held that the guarantees of the First Amendment, the prohibition against unreasonable searches and seizures of the Fourth Amendment, and the right to counsel guaranteed by the Sixth Amendment are all to be enforced against the States under the Fourteenth Amendment according to the same standards that protect those personal rights against federal encroachment"). In much the same way, the Fifth Amendment's understanding of due process includes an equal protection guarantee that the federal government must honor under the same standards, *Bolling v. Sharpe*, 347 U.S. 497, 499 (1954)("The Fifth Amendment ... does not contain an equal protection clause as does the Fourteenth Amendment which applies only to the states. But the concepts of equal protection and due process, both stemming from our American ideal of fairness, are not mutually exclusive. The 'equal protection of the laws' is a more explicit safeguard of prohibited unfairness than 'due process of law,' and therefore, we do not imply that the two are always interchangeable phrases. But, as this Court has recognized, discrimination may be so unjustifiable as to be violative of due process"); *Buckley v. Valeo*, 424 U.S. 1, 93 (1976)("Equal protection analysis in the Fifth Amendment area is the same as that under the Fourteenth Amendment").

[105] *First National Bank of Boston v. Bellotti*, 435 U.S. 765, 780 n.15 (1978), citing, *Santa Clara County v. Southern Pacific R. Co.*, 118 U.S. 394 (1886), and *Covington & Lexington Turnpike R. Co. v. Sandford*, 164 U.S. 578 (1896)("It has been settled for almost a century that corporations are persons within the meaning of the Fourteenth Amendment"); see also, *Grosjean v. American Press Co.*, 297 U.S. 233, 244 (1936)("But a corporation is a 'person' within the meaning of the equal protection and due process of law clauses.... ").

[106] *GSS Group Ltd v. National Port Authority*, 680 F.3d 805, 813 (D.C.Cir. 2012), citing inter alia, *Goodyear Dunlop Tires Operations, S.A. v. Brown*, 131 S.Ct. 2846, 2850-851 (2011); *J. McIntyre Mach., Ltd. v. Nicastro*, 131 S.Ct. 2780, 2785 (2011)("Both Supreme Court and this court have repeatedly held that foreign corporations may invoke due process protections to challenge the exercise of personal jurisdiction over them").

[107] *Chai v. Department of State*, 466 F.3d 125, 132 (D.C.Cir. 2006)(internal citations omitted).

[108] *South Carolina v. Katzenbach*, 383 U.S. 301, 323 (1966)("The word 'person' in the context of the Due Process Clause of the Fifth Amendment, cannot, by any reasonable mode of interpretation, be expanded to encompass the States of the Union, and to our knowledge this has never been done by any court"); see also, *South Dakota v. U.S. Dept. of Interior*, 665 F.3d 986, 990 (8th Cir. 2012).

[109] *GSS Group Ltd v. National Port Authority*, 680 F.3d at 809("[F]oreign sovereigns and their extensively-controlled instrumentalities are not 'persons' under the Fifth Amendment"); *Frontera Resources Azerbaijan v. State Oil*, 582 F.3d 393, 399 (2d Cir. 2009)("Neither States of the Union nor foreign nations are persons for Fifth Amendment purposes"); *Greater Heights Academy v. Zelman*, 522 F.3d 678, 681 (5th Cir. 2008)(political subdivisions of the states are not persons for due process purposes).

[110] *United States v. Hospital Monteflores, Inc.*, 575 F.2d 332, 335 (1st Cir. 1978); *United States v. Security National Bank*, 546 F.2d 492, 494 (2d Cir. 1976).

[111] *United States v. Martin Linen Supply Co.*, 430 U.S. 564 (1977); but also, *Eastern Enterprises v. Apfel*, 524 U.S. 498, 557 (1998)(Breyer, J., dissenting)(emphasis added)("Nor does application of the Due Process Clause automatically trigger the Takings Clause, just because the word 'property' appears in both. That word appears in the midst of different phrases with somewhat different objectives, thereby permitting differences in the way in which the term is interpreted. Compare, e.g., *United States v. Martin Linen Supply Co*, 430 U.S. 564 (1977) (*'person' includes corporations for purposes of Fifth Amendment Double Jeopardy Clause*), with *Doe v. United States*, 487 U.S. 201, 206 (1988) ('person' does not include a corporation for purposes of fifth Amendment Self-Incrimination Clause); *Strategic Defense International, Inc. v. United States*, 745 F.Supp.2d 1214, 1234 (S.D.Fla. 2010)(parallel citations omitted) ("Corporate identity has been determinative of whether a particular constitutional right is or is not available to a corporation.... *United States v. Martin Linen Supply*, 430 U.S. 564 (1977)(corporation protected against double jeopardy) ... ").

[112] U.S. Const. Amend. VI ("In all criminal prosecutions, the accused shall enjoy the right to a speedy and public trial, by an impartial jury of the State and district wherein the crime shall have been committed, which district shall have been previously ascertained by law, and to be informed of the nature and cause of the accusation; to be confronted with the witnesses against him; to have compulsory process for obtaining witnesses in his favor, and to have the Assistance of Counsel for his defense").

[113] *United States v. Rad-O-Lite of Philadelphia, Inc.*, 612 F.2d 740, 743 (3d Cir. 1979)("The sixth amendment describes the class of persons protected by its terms with the word 'accused.' This language does not suggest that the protection of sixth amendment rights is restricted to individual defendants").

[114] *United States v. Unimex, Inc.*, 991 F.2d 546, 549-51(9th Cir. 1993); *United States v. Rad-O-Lite of Philadelphia, Inc.*, 612 F.2d at 743; see also, *American Airways Charters, Inc. v. Regan*, 746 F.2d 865, 873 n.14 (D.C.Cir. 1984("It appears beyond sensible debate that corporations, in our society, do indeed enjoy the right to retain counsel. Corporations may not assert 'purely personal' rights but, no less than natural persons, they are entitled to due process and the equal protection of the laws.... [T]he right to effective assistance of counsel is not so peculiarly applicable to individuals that corporations should not be entitled to it. In fact, denying a corporation the right to retain counsel may be tantamount to stripping the corporation of its right to defend itself in court, for it is established that a corporation, which is an artificial entity that can only act through agents, cannot proceed pro se").

[115] *United States v. Hartsell*, 127 F.3d 343, 350 (4th Cir. 1997); *United States v. Unimex, Inc.*, 991 F.2d at 550; *United States v. Rivera*, 912 F.Supp. 634, 638 (D.P.R. 1966).

[116] U.S. Const. Amend. VI.

[117] "The indictment or information must be a plain, concise, and definite written state of the essential facts constituting the offense charged.... " F.R.Crim.Pro. 7(c)(1); e.g., *United States v. Triumph Capital Group, Inc.*, 360 F.Supp.2d 470, 474-74 (D.Conn. 2004).

[118] *Rideau v. Louisiana*, 373 U.S. 723,726-27 (1963); *Estes v. Texas*, 381 U.S. 532, 538-40 (1965).

[119] *Presley v. Georgia*, 558 U.S. 209, 212 (2010).

[120] *Vermont v. Brillon*, 556 U.S. 81, 88 (2009), quoting, *Barker v. Wingo*, 407 U.S. 514, 530 (1972).

[121] *United States v. Litton Systems, Inc.*, 722 F.2d 264, 265-66 (5th Cir. 1984); *United States v. Sears, Roebuck and Co., Inc.*, 877 F.2d 734, 739 (9th Cir. 1989).

[122] *Muniz v. Hoffman*, 422 U.S. 454, 477 (1975)(a $10,000 fine imposed upon a large union did not trigger the jury trial right); *United Mine Workers v. Bagwell*, 512 U.S. 821, 824, 838 (1994)($64 million in fines does trigger a jury trial right); *Southern Union Co. v. United States*, 132 S.Ct. 2344, (2012)("The RCRA subjects Southern Union to a maximum fine of

$50,000 for each of violation. 42 U.S.C. 6928(d). The Government does not deny that, in light of the seriousness of that punishment, the company was properly accorded a jury trial. And the Government now concedes the District Court made factual findings that increased both the 'potential and actual' fine the court imposed. This is exactly what *Apprendi* guards against: judicial factfinding that enlarges the maximum punishment a defendant faces beyond what the jury's verdict or the defendant's admissions allow").

[123] U.S. Const. Art. III, §2, cl. 3 ("The trial of all Crimes ... shall be held in the State where the said Crimes shall have been committed ... "); Amend. VI ("In all criminal prosecutions, the accused shall enjoy the right to ... a trial, by an impartial jury of the State and district wherein the crime shall have been committed ...").

[124] *United States v. Oceanpro Industries, Ltd.*, 674 F.3d 323, 327-30 (4th Cir. 2012); *United States v. Canal Barge Co., Inc.*, 631 F.3d 347, 351-54 (6th Cir. 2011); *United States v. Beech-Nut Nutrition Corp.*, 871 F.2d 1181, 1188-191 (2d Cir. 1989)—each citing as authority cases that only human defendants.

[125] U.S. Const. Amend. VI.

[126] *Williams v. Illinois*, 132 S.Ct. 2221, 2232 (2012), quoting, 541 U.S. 36, 59 (2004).

[127] *Taylor v. Illinois*, 484 U.S. 400, 408 (1988), quoting, *Pennsylvania v. Ritchie*, 480 U.S. 39, 56 (1987).

[128] *Perry v. New Hampshire*, 132 S.Ct. 726, 723 (2012)(internal citations omitted)("The Constitution ... protects a defendant against a conviction based on evidence of questionable reliability, not by prohibiting introduction of the evidence, but by affording the defendant means to persuade the jury that the evidence should be discounted as unworthy of credit. Constitutional safeguards available to defendants to counter the State's evidence include ... compulsory process and confrontation plus cross-examination of witnesses"); *Taylor v. Illinois*, 484 U.S. at 408 ("Indeed, this right [to compulsory process] is an essential attribute of the adversary system itself").

[129] *United States v. Nippon Paper Industries Co., Ltd.*, 17 F.Supp.2d 38, 40 (D.Mass. 1998)(right to confrontation); *United States v. Nebraska Beef, Ltd.*, 194 F.Supp.2d 949, (D.Neb. 2002)(compulsory process).

[130] *United States v. Bajakajian*, 524 U.S. 321, 334 (1998).

[131] *United States v. Chaplin's, Inc.*, 646 F.3d 846, 851 n.15 (11th Cir. 2011), citing, *Browning-Ferris v. Kelco Disposal, Inc.*, 492 U.S. 257, 276 n.22 (1989).

[132] *United States v. Jalaram, Inc.*, 599 F.3d 347, 357 (4th Cir. 2010).

[133] Of course, government action, public scorn, or the two in concert may wipe them out of existence.

[134] Cf., 18 U.S.C. 3571 (designating maximum fines for organizations convicted of felonies and various misdemeanors).

[135] Cf., 18 U.S.C. 3561(a)(1)(noting that all defendants may be placed on probation other than individuals convicted of class A or B felonies); U.S.S.G. §8D1.1.

[136] Cf., U.S.S.G. §8B1.1. The statutes that authorize restitution orders refer to simply to "victims" or "defendants" rather than to "individuals," "organizations," or "corporations," 18 U.S.C. 3663, 3663A, 2248, 2259, 2264, 2327.

[137] Cf., U.S.S.G. §§8E1.2, 5E1.4.

[138] *Gall v. United States*, 552 U.S. 38, 49 (2007)("[A] district court should begin all sentencing proceedings by correctly calculating the applicable Guidelines range. As a matter of administration and to secure nationwide consistency, the Guidelines should be the starting point and the initial benchmark"); *United States v. Goodwin*, 717 F.3d 511, 520(7th Cir. 2013).

[139] *Gall v. United States*, 552 U.S. at 49-50.

[140] *Gall v. United States*, 552 U.S. at 51; *United States v. Douglas*, 713 F.3d 694, 700 (2d Cir. 2013).

[141] *Gall v. United States*, 552 U.S. at 51; *United States v. Alvarado*, 720 F.3d 153, 157 (2d Cir. 2013)("A district court errs procedurally when it fails to calculate (or improperly calculates)

the Sentencing Guidelines range, treats the Sentencing Guidelines as mandatory, fails to consider the §3553(a) factors, selects a sentence based on clearly erroneous facts, or fails adequately to explain the chosen sentence"); *United States v. Sandoval-Orellana*, 714 F.3d 1174, 1180 (9th Cir. 2013).

142 *United States v. Douglas*, 713 F.3d at 700 (We set aside a district court's sentence as substantively unreasonable only if affirming it would damage the administration of justice because the sentence imposed was shockingly high, shockingly low, or otherwise unsupportable as a matter of law"); *United States v. Ciavarella*, 716 F.3d 705, 735 n.19 (3d Cir. 2013)("In evaluating the substantive reasonableness of a sentence, we consider whether the record as a whole reflects rational and meaningful consideration of the factors enumerated in 18 U.S.C. §3553(a)").

143 U.S.S.G. §8C1.1. The Guidelines, however, operate within the confines established by Congress. The Guideline calculation that falls short of a statutory minimum or exceeds a statutory maximum must be adjusted accordingly, U.S.S.G. §§8C3.1, 5E1.2(c).

144 U.S.S.G. §8C1.1. *United States v. Najjar*, 300 F.3d 466, (4th Cir. 2002)("Tri-City was exposed to a $500,000 fine under the statute and what has been called a death penalty fine under §8C1.1 of the Sentencing Guidelines.... It is clear that Tri-City was conceived in crime and performed little or no legitimate activity ").

145 18 U.S.C. 3572(b); U.S.S.G. §8C2.2.

146 U.S.S.G. §8C2.1 ("The provisions of §§8C2.2 through 8C2.9 apply to each count for which the applicable guideline offense level is determined under: §§2B1.1[theft], 2B1.4[insider trading], 2B2.3[trespass], 2B4.1[commercial bribery], 2B5.3[copyright or trademark infringement], 2B6.1[vehicle identification numbers]; §§2C1.1[bribery], 2C1.2[illegal gratuity], 2C1.6 [deleted]; §§2D1.7[sale of drug paraphernalia], 2D3.1[controlled substance regulatory offenses], 2D3.2[same]; §§2E3.1[gambling], 2E4.1[contraband tobacco products], 2E5.1[labor racketeering], 2E5.3[labor record false statements]; §2G3.1[dealing in obscenity]; §§2K1.1[failure to report stolen explosives], 2K2.1[unlawful firearms transactions]; §2L1.1[smuggling]; §2N3.1[odometer offenses]; §2R1.1[antitrust]; §§2S1.1[money laundering], 2S1.3[smurfing]; §§2T1.1[tax evasion], 2T1.4[tax fraud principal], 2T1.6[failure to collect taxes], 2T1.7[failure to deposit collected taxes], 2T1.8[withholding offenses], 2T1.9[tax conspiracy], 2T2.1[nonpayment of alcohol tax], 2T2.2[regulatory tax offenses], 2T3.1[evade customs duties]; or when one of these guidelines is determinative, §§2E1.1[racketeering], 2X1.1[attempt or conspiracy], 2X2.1 [aiding and abetting], 2X3.1[accessory after the fact], 2X4.1[misprision of a felony]").

147 U.S.S.G. §8C2.10, *Background* ("The Commission has not promulgated guidelines governing the setting of fines for counts not covered by §8C2.1").

148 U.S.S.G. §8C2.10.

149 As a general rule, a court may impose a fine of not more than $500,000 when an organization is convicted of a felony, and a fine for misdemeanors ranging from not more than $10,000 to not more than $500,000, 18 U.S.C. 3571(c). These general limitations notwithstanding, a court may impose a fine of not more than twice the gain or loss associated with the offense, 18 U.S.C. 3571(c), (d), and may impose higher fines when Congress has authorized them for a specific crime, 18 U.S.C. 3571(c)(1).

150 18 U.S.C. 3553.

151 *United State v. Iona Management S.A.*, 555 F.3d 303, 310 (2d Cir. 2009)(emphasis added)("Iona primarily argues that the District Court erred in its grouping analysis by not following Sentencing Guidelines Section 3D1.2. The District Court, however, was not sentencing pursuant to this section, and was not required to do so because *there were no guidelines applicable to the organizational offense at issue*. Accordingly, the District Court 'determine[d] an appropriate fine by applying the provisions 18 U.S.C. §§3553 and 3572'"); but see, 18 U.S.C. 3553(a)(4)(".... The court, in determining the particular sentence to be imposed, shall consider ... (4) ... the sentencing range established for—(A) the applicable

category of offense committed by the applicable category of defendants as set forth in the [sentencing] guidelines ... ").

[152] U.S.S.G. §8C2.2; *United States v. Patient Transfer Service, Inc.*, 413 F.3d 734, 745 (8th Cir. 2005).

[153] U.S.S.G. §8C2.3 to §8C2.9.

[154] U.S.S.G. §8C2.3(a)("For each count covered by §8C2.1 (Applicability of Fine Guidelines), use the applicable Chapter Two guideline to determine the base offense level and apply, in the order listed, any appropriate adjustments contained in that [Chapter Two] guideline").

[155] U.S.S.G. §8C2.4. For example, a corporation, Bio-Med Plus Inc., and its operators were recently convicted of mail fraud, wire fraud, money laundering and racketeering in connection with a large scale Medicaid scheme, *United States v. Brady*, 644 F.3d, 1213, 1302 (11th Cir. 2011). Mail or wire fraud convictions begin with a base offense level of 6, U.S.S.G. §2B1.1(a)(2). The fraud Guideline calls for additional offense levels based on the amount of the property involved in the fraud. In the Bio-Med case, the scheme involved over $33 million, hence an addition of 22 levels to an offense level of 28, U.S.S.G. §2B1.1(b)(1)(L). A fraud with multiple victims warrants a higher offense level, U.S.S.G. §2B1.1(b)(2)(B). Bio-Med's offense level grew by 4 levels to an offense level of 32 because its fraudulent scheme victimized from than 50 individuals or entities. The receipt of stolen property (+2 offense levels, U.S.S.G. §2B1.1(b)(4)) and sophisticated attempts to avoid detection (+2 offense levels, U.S.S.G. §2B1.1(b)(10)), attributed to the plot, produced a final offense level of 36. The final offense level gave the court a starting point for its calculation of the fine to be imposed as discussed below.

[156] U.S.S.G. §§8C2.5 to 8C2.8.

[157] U.S.S.G. §8C2.5(a).

[158] Points are added for (1) the corporation's involvement in or tolerance of criminal conduct, (2) its history of misconduct, and (3) its involvement in any obstruction of justice; points are subtracted if the corporation has an effective compliance program, and for its acceptance of responsibility, cooperation with authorities, or self-disclosure of criminal misconduct, U.S.S.G. §§8C2.5(b) to 8C1.5(g).

[159] U.S.S.G. §8C2.6.

[160] *Id.* In the Bio-Med case noted above, "[t]he district court reached a culpability score of 10 based on: (1) a starting score of five pursuant to §8C2.5(a); (2) an increase of two pursuant to §8C2.5(b)(4) because Bio-Med had fifty or more employees, at least one of whom had substantial authority to act on behalf of the organization and participated in, condoned, or was willfully ignorant of the criminal conduct; and (3) an increase of three pursuant to §8C2.5(e) because Bradley III. on behalf of Bio-Med, obstructed justice. A score of 10 corresponds to a minimum multiplier of 2.00 and a maximum of 4.00. A total offense level of 36 corresponds to a fine amount of $45.5 million.... Accordingly, the Guidelines fine range for Bio-Med came to between $91 million and $182 million," *United States v. Bradley*, 644 F.3d 1213, 1303 (11th Cir. 2011).

[161] U.S.S.G. §8C2.8("(a) In determining the amount of the fine within the applicable guideline range, the court should consider: (1) the need for the sentence to reflect the seriousness of the offense, promote respect for the law, provide just punishment, afford adequate deterrence, and protect the public from further crimes of the organization; (2) the organization's role in the offense; (3) any collateral consequences of conviction, including civil obligations arising from the organization's conduct; (4) any nonpecuniary loss caused or threatened by the offense; (5) whether the offense involved a vulnerable victim; (6) any prior criminal record of an individual within high-level personnel of the organization or high-level personnel of a unit of the organization who participated in, condoned, or was willfully ignorant of the criminal conduct; (7) any prior civil or criminal misconduct by the organization other than that counted under §8C2.5(c); (8) any culpability score under §8C2.5(Culpability Score) higher than 10 or lower than 0; (9) partial but incomplete satisfaction of the conditions for one or more of the mitigating or aggravating factors set for

in §8C2.5 (Culpability Score); (10) any factor listed in 18 U.S.C. §3572(a); and (11) whether the organization failed to have, at the time of the instance offense, an effective compliance and ethics program within the meaning of §8B2.1 (Effective Compliance and Ethics Program). (b) In addition, the court may consider the relative importance of any factor used to determine the range, including the pecuniary loss caused by the offense, the pecuniary gain from the offense, any specific offense characteristic used to determine the offense level, and any aggravating or mitigating factor used to determine the culpability score").

[162] U.S.S.G. §8C3.1(b), (c).

[163] U.S.S.G. §8C2.9.

[164] U.S.S.G. §8C3.3.

[165] U.S.S.G. §8C3.4.

[166] U.S.S.C. §8C4.2.

[167] U.S.S.C. §8C4.3.

[168] U.S.S.C. §8C4.4.

[169] U.S.S.C. §8C4.5.

[170] U.S.S.C. §8C4.6.

[171] U.S.S.C. §8C4.10.

[172] U.S.S.C. §8C4.11.

[173] U.S.S.C. §8C4.1.

[174] U.S.S.C. §8C4.7.

[175] U.S.S.C. §8C4.8.

[176] U.S.S.C. §8C4.9.

[177] U.S.S.G. §8D1.1(a)(7); 18 U.S.C. 3551(c).

[178] *Id.*

[179] U.S.S.G. §8D1.2(a); 18 U.S.C. 3561(c)(but for not more than one year if the corporation is convicted of an infraction rather than a felony or misdemeanor).

[180] U.S.S.G. §8D1.2(a)(1); 18 U.S.C. 3561(c)(1).

[181] U.S.S.G. §8D1.1(a)(1), (2), (3).

[182] U.S.S.G. §8D1.1(a)(4).

[183] U.S.S.G. §8D1.1(a)(5).

[184] U.S.S.G. §8D1.1(a)(6).

[185] U.S.S.G. §8D1.1(a)(4); 18 U.S.C. 3553(a)(2).

[186] 18 U.S.C. 3563(a)(1), U.S.S.G. §8D1.3(a)(1). In the case of a felony conviction and in the absence of extraordinary circumstances, however, the court must require the corporation either to make restitution and do community service. Under extraordinary circumstances, the court may substitute one of the standard discretionary conditions in lieu of restitution or community service, 18 U.S.C. 3563(a)(2), U.S.S.G. §8D1.3(a)(2).

[187] U.S.S.G. §8D1.4(a).

[188] U.S.S.G. §8D1.4(b)(1).

[189] U.S.S.G. §8D1.4(b)(2).

[190] U.S.S.G. §8D1.4(b)(4), (3).

[191] U.S.S.G. §8D1.4(b)(5).

[192] U.S.S.G. §8D1.4(b)(6).

[193] 18 U.S.C. 3563(b)(22); U.S.S.G. §8D1.3(c).

[194] 18 U.S.C. 3565(a); U.S.S.G. §8F1.1.

[195] 18 U.S.C. 3013; U.S.S.G. §8E1.1.

[196] See generally CRS Report RL34138, *Restitution in Federal Criminal Cases.*

[197] 18 U.S.C. 3663A(c)(i); U.S.S.G. §8B1.1(a)(1).

[198] 18 U.S.C. 3663A(c)(ii); U.S.S.G. §8B1.1(a)(1).

[199] 18 U.S.C. 3663A(c)(ii); 21 U.S.C. 856; U.S.S.G. §8B1.1(a)(1).

[200] 18 U.S.C. 3663A(c)(iii); U.S.S.G. §8B1.1(a)(1).

[201] *Id.*

[202] 18 U.S.C. 2248; U.S.S.G. §8B1.1(a)(1).

[203] 18 U.S.C. 2259; U.S.S.G. §8B1.1(a)(1).

[204] 18 U.S.C. 2264; U.S.S.G. §8B1.1(a)(1). Although it seems unlikely that some of these offenses would be committed the benefit of a corporation thus triggering corporate liability, the Guidelines list them among the offenses for which corporate restitution must be imposed in section 8B1.1(a)(1).

[205] 18 U.S.C. 2327; U.S.S.G. §8B1.1(a)(1).

[206] 18 U.S.C. 228(d).

[207] 18 U.S.C. 2323(c).

[208] 21 U.S.C. 853(q).

[209] 18 U.S.C. 1593.

[210] 18 U.S.C. 3663(a)(1)(A); U.S.S.G. §8B1.1(a)(1). The Guidelines group the offenses triggering discretionary restitution with those triggering mandatory restitution , U.S.S.G. §8B1.1(a)(1)("(a) In the case of an identifiable victim, the court shall offenses—(1) enter a restitution order for the full amount of the victim's loss, if such order is authorized under 18 U.S.C.... §3663, or §3663A").

[211] 18 U.S.C. 3663(a)(1); 49 U.S.C. 5124.

[212] 18 U.S.C. 3663(a)(1); 49 U.S.C. 46312.

[213] 18 U.S.C. 3663(a)(1); 49 U.S.C. 46502.

[214] 18 U.S.C. 3663(a)(1); 49 U.S.C. 46504.

[215] 18 U.S.C. 3663(a)(1).

[216] 18 U.S.C. 3563(b)(2).

[217] 18 U.S.C. 3663(a)(1)(A), (3).

[218] 18 U.S.C. 3555; U.S.S.G. §§8B1.4, 5F1.4.

[219] U.S.S.G. §8B2.1(a).

[220] U.S.S.G. §8D2.1(b)(1): "Due diligence and the promotion of an organizational culture that encourages ethical conduct and a commitment to compliance with the law within the meaning of subsection (a) minimally require the following: (1) The organization shall establish standards and procedures to prevent and detect criminal conduct."

[221] U.S.S.G. §8D2.1(b)(2): "(A) The organization's governing authority shall be knowledgeable about the content and operation of the compliance and ethics program and shall exercise reasonable oversight with respect to the implementation and effectiveness of the compliance and ethics program. (B) High-level personnel of the organization shall ensure that the organization has an effective compliance and ethics program, as described in this guideline. Specific individual(s) within high-level personnel shall be assigned overall responsibility for the compliance and ethics program. (C) Specific individual(s) within the organization shall be delegated day-to-day operational responsibility for the compliance and ethics program. Individual(s) with operational responsibility shall report periodically to high-level personnel and, as appropriate, to the governing authority, or an appropriate subgroup of the governing authority, on the effectiveness of the compliance and ethics program. To carry out such operational responsibility, such individual(s) shall be given adequate resources, appropriate authority, and direct access to the governing authority or an appropriate subgroup of the governing authority."

[222] U.S.S.G. §8D2.1(b)(3): "The organization shall use reasonable efforts not to include within the substantial authority personnel of the organization any individual whom the organization knew, or should have known through the exercise of due diligence, has engaged in illegal activities or other conduct inconsistent with an effective compliance and ethics program."

[223] U.S.S.G. §8D2.1(b)(4): "(A) The organization shall take reasonable steps to communicate periodically and in a practical manner its standards and procedures, and other aspects of the compliance and ethics program, to the individuals referred to in subparagraph (B) by conducting effective training programs and otherwise disseminating information appropriate to such individuals' respective roles and responsibilities. (B) The individuals referred to in

subparagraph (A) are the members of the governing authority, high-level personnel, substantial authority personnel, the organization's employees, and, as appropriate, the organization's agents."

[224] U.S.S.G. §8D2.1(b)(5): "The organization shall take reasonable steps—(A) to ensure that the organization's compliance and ethics program is followed, including monitoring and auditing to detect criminal conduct; (B) to evaluate periodically the effectiveness of the organization's compliance and ethics program; and (C) to have and publicize a system, which may include mechanisms that allow for anonymity or confidentiality, whereby the organization's employees and agents may report or seek guidance regarding potential or actual criminal conduct without fear of retaliation." See also, U.S.S.G. §8D2.1(c): "In implementing subsection (b), the organization shall periodically assess the risk of criminal conduct and shall take appropriate steps to design, implement, or modify each requirement set forth in subsection (b) to reduce the risk of criminal conduct identified through this process."

[225] U.S.S.G. §8D2.1(b)(6): "The organization's compliance and ethics program shall be promoted and enforced consistently throughout the organization through (A) appropriate incentives to perform in accordance with the compliance and ethics program; and (B) appropriate disciplinary measures for engaging in criminal conduct and for failing to take reasonable steps to prevent or detect criminal conduct."

[226] U.S.S.G. §8D2.1(b)(7): "After criminal conduct has been detected, the organization shall take reasonable steps to respond appropriately to the criminal conduct and to prevent further similar criminal conduct, including making any necessary modifications to the organization's compliance and ethics program."

[227] U.S.S.G. §8D1.3; U.S.S.G. §8D1.3 (*Commentary*).

[228] U.S.S.G. §8D1.3 (*Commentary*).

[229] U.S.S.G. §8D1.2.

[230] See generally CRS Report 97-139, *Crime and Forfeiture.*

[231] E.g., 18 U.S.C. 981 (civil forfeiture), 982 (criminal forfeiture); *Austin v. United States*, 509 U.S. 602, 622 (1993).

[232] U.S.S.G. §§8E1.2, 5E1.4.

In: Corporate Criminal Liability
Editor: Brandon P. Burton

ISBN: 978-1-63117-724-8

Chapter 2

PROSECUTORIAL DISCRETION IN THE CONTEXT OF CORPORATE ATTORNEY-CLIENT RELATIONS*

Charles Doyle

SUMMARY

The Justice Department enjoys prosecutorial discretion to bring criminal charges against a corporation, its culpable officers or employees, or both. For a corporation, indictment alone can be catastrophic, if not fatal, in some instances. The Thompson Memorandum, since replaced with guidelines in the U. S. Attorneys Manual, described the policy factors to be considered in the exercise of prosecutorial discretion. Two of the factors explicitly mentioned were whether a corporation had waived its privileges and whether it had cut off the payment of attorneys' fees for its officers and employees.

Justice Department policies and practices under the Thompson Memorandum led to constitutional challenges based on the Fifth Amendment's self-incrimination clause, the Amendment's due process clause, and the Sixth Amendment's right to counsel clause. Due process and right to counsel concerns were enough for a federal district court in New York to throw out the indictments of thirteen former partners and employees of an accounting firm, charged with creating and marketing

---

* This is an edited, reformatted and augmented version of Congressional Research Service Publication, No. RL33842, dated March 9, 2010.

fraudulent tax shelters, *United States v. Stein.* The Second Circuit affirmed on right to counsel grounds and consequently found it necessary to address the merits of the due process argument.

The House addressed the conflict in attorney-client protective legislation which it passed in the 110th Congress. Soon thereafter, the Department of Justice announced a revised policy concerning the circumstances under which a corporation's failure to waive its attorney-client privilege might influence the decision to prosecute it. The 110th Congress, which had previously amended the Federal Rules of Evidence relating to the inadvertent waiver of the attorney-client privilege, adjourned without taking further action on the House-passed legislation. Similar proposals, however, have been introduced in 111th Congress, H.R. 4326 (Representative Scott); S. 445 (Senator Specter). This report provides a brief discussion of the legislation, the legal background, and a chronology of related issues and events.

INTRODUCTION

A corporation is subject to civil and criminal liability for the misconduct that its officers, employees, and agents committed for its benefit.[1] Federal authorities may prosecute a corporation; its officers, employees, and agents; or both.[2] For a corporation, however, indictment can be fatal. Commentators point to the experience of the Arthur Andersen accounting firm as evidence that some companies cannot survive the mere accusation of criminal wrongdoing, even if they might have been vindicated ultimately.[3]

Under most circumstances, corporations and their servants alike enjoy the right to attorney-client privileges and to attorney work product protection in connection with government investigations of possible misconduct.[4] Yet, the Justice Department's federal prosecution policy at one time suggested that a corporation faced an increased risk of prosecution, if it claimed those privileges or if it paid the business-related litigation costs of its officers and employees.

The federal courts in at least one circuit have concluded that the manner in which the policy (the so-called Thompson Memorandum) was implemented contravened the dictates of the Fifth and Sixth Amendments.[5]

Both Houses held hearings on the matter during the 109th Congress and the 110th Congress.[6] The House Judiciary Committee reported out the Attorney-Client Privilege Protection Act of 2007,[7] which the House passed under suspension of the rules on November 13, 2007.[8] Soon thereafter, the Department of Justice announced a revised policy concerning the circumstances under which a corporation's failure to waive its attorney-client privilege might influence the decision to prosecute it.[9] The 110th Congress concluded without further action, although a related amendment to the Federal Rules of Evidence did pass.[10] Proposals similar to that passed by the House in the 110th Congress have been introduced in the 111th Congress, H.R. 4326 (Representative Scott); S. 445 (Senator Specter).

ENTERPRISE LIABILITY

At common law, corporations were considered incapable of committing or of being punished for criminal misconduct.[11] That perception has changed, however. Corporate criminal liability is now a matter of legislative choice. And the view of the courts is much the same as it was over a century ago, when the Supreme Court observed:

> We see no valid objection in law, and every reason in public policy, why the corporation which profits by the transaction, and can only act through its agents and officers, shall be held punishable by fine because of the knowledge and intent of its agents to whom it has intrusted authority to act in the subject-matter of making and fixing rates of transportation, and whose knowledge and purposes may well be attributed to the corporation for which the agents act. While the law should have regard to the rights of all, and to those of corporations no less than to those of individuals, it cannot shut its eyes to the fact that the great majority of business transactions in modern times are conducted through those bodies, and particularly that interstate commerce is almost entirely in their hands, and to give them immunity from all punishment because of the old and exploded doctrine that corporation cannot commit a crime would virtually take away the only means of effectually controlling the subject-matter and correcting the abuses aimed at. *New York Central R.R. v. United States*, 212 U.S. 481, 495-96 (1909).

Both as a general matter and within individual criminal statutes, federal law leaves little doubt when a criminal proscription applies to corporate entities. The Dictionary Act provides that "[i]n determining the meaning of any Act of Congress, unless the context indicates otherwise ... the words 'person' or 'whoever' include corporations, companies, associations, firms, partnerships, societies, and joint stock companies, as well as individuals."[12] With this in mind, criminal statutes ordinarily condemn—"whoever," or any "person" who—engages in the misconduct they proscribe.[13] In some instances, the statute goes a step further and supplies an even more expansive crime-specific definition.[14]

When a federal criminal statute applies to corporations, the courts have generally said that a corporation is liable for the violations committed for its benefit by its officers, employees, or agents acting, within the apparent scope of their authority,[15] even if the corporation has either generally or specifically prohibited the misconduct in question.[16] Of course, the officers, employees, or agents whose misconduct is imputed to the corporation are usually subject to criminal liability as well.[17] It is a matter of prosecutorial discretion whether to prosecute an apparently culpable corporation, or its apparently culpable agents, employees, and officers, or both the corporation and the individuals through whom it has acted.[18] Because their interests are intertwined, corporations often bear the legal costs of defending their agents, employees, and officers in litigation arising out of conduct within the apparent scope of their employment.[19] The corporation in such cases, however, is generally entitled to reimbursement should its agent, officer or employee be convicted or otherwise found at fault.[20]

ATTORNEY-CLIENT PRIVILEGE AND WORK PRODUCT PROTECTION

The attorney-client privilege and work product protection are federal evidentiary privileges, which means they are "governed by the principles of the common law as ... interpreted by the courts of the United States in light of reason and experience," F.R.Evid. 501, unless altered by rule or statute.

Attorney-Client

The attorney-client privilege is one of the oldest common law privileges.[21] The purpose of the privilege is to encourage "full and frank communication between attorneys and their clients and thereby promote broader public interests in the observance of law and the administration of justice."[22] It protects confidential communications with an attorney made in order to obtain legal advice or assistance.[23]

It is available to corporations as well as to individuals.[24] In the case of a corporation, it now seems beyond dispute that the privilege applies to the confidential communications from its officers, agents, and employees to its attorney for the purpose of supplying the corporation with legal advice or assistance.[25] At one time, however, some courts believed the privilege should be limited to the communications of the "control group of the corporation," those ultimately responsible for corporate policy. The Supreme Court in *Upjohn* found this reading too limited.[26]

The case began when officials at Upjohn became concerned that some of its officers or employees might have been involved in the business-related bribery of foreign officials.[27] Upjohn's general counsel was instructed to conduct an investigation.[28] Following the internal investigation, Upjohn reported suspicious payments to the Securities and Exchange Commission (SEC) and the Internal Revenue Service (IRS).[29] The company also identified which of its officers and employees had been interviewed or had submitted responses to questionnaires as part of the internal investigation.[30] Then the IRS issued a summons demanding that Upjohn turn over all its files on the internal investigation including responses to its general counsel's questionnaires and memoranda and to notes of the investigation's interviews conducted under his supervision.[31] Upjohn refused to comply, claiming attorney-client and attorney work product privileges, and the IRS sought judicial enforcement of its summons.[32]

The Sixth Circuit Court of Appeals rejected Upjohn's attorney-client claim on the grounds that the communications sought were not those of Upjohn's control group, thus not those of the client, and therefore not privileged.[33] The Supreme Court found this control group test insufficiently protective. The test failed to recognize the importance of the attorney's fact gathering communications with the corporation's employees conducted in order to provide the corporate client with legal advice or assistance.[34] In doing so, it frustrated the very purpose of the privilege by discouraging full and frank disclosures by those associated with the company who were in a position to expose it to civil and criminal liability, thereby denying counsel the basis for sound legal advice and assistance.[35] Moreover, it chilled communications between counsel and company employees designed to ensure company compliance with the law.[36]

In a situation like the one in *Upjohn*, the attorney represents the corporation, the privilege that envelops the communications with the attorney belongs to the corporation,[37] and may be waived by the corporation.[38] Although disclosure ordinarily waives the privilege, the circuits are divided over whether the privilege may survive disclosure for limited selective purposes (selective waiver) such as the disclosures in *Upjohn* to government investigators or regulators.[39]

The prospect of selective waiver was apparently first raised in *Diversified Industries v. Meredith*, where the Eighth Circuit held voluntary disclosure to the Securities and Exchange Commission (SEC) did not constitute a waiver of the privilege for subsequent purposes.[40] To one extent or another, the District of Columbia, First, Second, Third, Fourth and Tenth Circuits have declined to accept the Eighth Circuit suggestion that the attorney-client privilege may be claimed following a selective disclosure to a governmental agency.[41]

The existence of either a common interest or joint defense attorney-client privilege further complicates matters, for either may arise in the course of an investigation of allegations of corporate misconduct. The common interest privilege is created when an attorney simultaneously represents more than one client based on their common interest in the same matter. Under such circumstances, "communications between each of the clients and the attorney are privileged against third parties, and it is unnecessary that there be actual litigation in progress for this privilege to apply."[42] Moreover, two or more clients represented by individual attorneys may agree to work jointly in a common defense of a particular suit or case. In such circumstances, "many courts have held that the attorney-client privilege gives rise to a concomitant 'joint defense privilege' which serves to protect the confidentiality of communications, passing from one party to the attorney for another party where a joint defense effort or strategy has been decided upon and undertaken by the parties and their respective counsel."[43] The courts have generally held— although not universally so—that communications or attorney work product protected by a joint or common defense privileges can only be waived with the consent of all parties.[44]

Attorney Work Product

At least since the Supreme Court announced its decision in *Hickman v. Taylor*,[45] the federal courts have recognized that an attorney's work product gathered or created in anticipation of litigation enjoys qualified disclosure protection. The protection has been reenforced by rule both on the civil side[46] and in criminal cases.[47]

"At its core, the work-product doctrine shelters the mental processes of the attorney providing a privileged area within which he can analyze and prepare his client's case.... It is therefore necessary that the doctrine protect material prepared by agents of the attorney as well as those prepared by the attorney himself."[48]

The protection can be waived,[49] but here too the circuits are divided on the question of whether it can survive a selective waiver in the form of disclosure to a government investigator or regulator. The Fourth Circuit and Federal Circuit have been unwilling to say that the protection afforded attorney opinion work product (work containing the attorney's analysis of the law, facts, and strategy reflecting the attorney's mental impressions)[50] is lost simply because it has been disclosed to governmental entities.[51] On the other hand, the Third Circuit has said without equivocation that the same standard used in the case of attorney-client waivers should apply; that is, disclosure to a governmental entity constitutes complete waiver.[52] The other circuits that have considered the question have assumed positions at various points between the two.[53]

DEPUTY ATTORNEY GENERAL MEMORANDA AND RELATED MATTERS

Five Deputy Attorneys General have issued memoranda to guide the exercise of prosecutorial discretion on the question of whether criminal charges should be brought against a corporation. Each includes provisions concerning the waiver of attorney-client and attorney work product protection, and all but one address employee legal costs and joint defense agreements as well. They are the memoranda of: Deputy Attorney Generals Holder,[54] Thompson,[55] McNulty,[56] and Filip[57] and Acting Deputy Attorney General McCallum.[58]

Holder Memorandum

Signed on June 19, 1999, the Holder Memorandum was designed to provide prosecutors with factors to be considered when determining whether to charge a corporation with criminal activity. It emphasized that "[t]hese factors are, however, not outcome-determinative and are only guidelines."

The factors consisted of: "1. The nature and seriousness of the offense. . . 2. The pervasiveness of wrongdoing within the corporation. . . 3. The corporation's history of similar conduct. . . 4. The corporation's timely and voluntary disclosure of wrongdoing and its willingness to cooperate in the investigation of its agents. . . 5. The existence and adequacy of the corporation's compliance program. . . 6. The corporation's remedial actions. . . 7. Collateral consequences ... and 8. The adequacy of non-criminal remedies. . . ."[59]

In the section devoted to cooperation and voluntary disclosure, the Memorandum stated that "In gauging the extent of the corporation's cooperation, the prosecutor may consider the corporation's willingness ... to waive the attorney-client and work product privileges."[60] As the Comment that followed explained:

> One factor the prosecutor may weigh in assessing the adequacy of a corporation's cooperation is the completeness of its disclosure including, if necessary, a waiver of the attorney-client and work product protections, both with respect to its internal investigation and with respect to communications between specific officers, directors, and employees and counsel. Such waivers permit the government to obtain statements of possible witnesses, subjects, and targets, without having to negotiate individual cooperation or immunity agreements. In addition, they are often critical in enabling the government to evaluate the completeness of a corporation's voluntary disclosure and cooperation. Prosecutors, may, therefore, request a waiver in appropriate circumstances. [This waiver should ordinarily be limited to the factual internal investigation and any contemporaneous advice given to the corporation concerning the conduct at issue. Except in unusual circumstances, prosecutors should not seek a waiver with respect to communications and work product related to advice concerning the government's criminal investigation.] The Department does not, however, consider waiver of a corporation's privileges an absolute requirement, and prosecutor should consider the willingness of a corporation to waive the privileges when necessary to provide timely and complete information as only one factor in evaluating the corporation's cooperation. Holder Memorandum, VI. B. (Memorandum's footnote appears in brackets).

The Memorandum also addressed the adverse weight that might be given a corporation's participation in a joint defense agreement with its officers or employees and its agreement to pay their legal fees:

> Another factor to be weighed by the prosecutor is whether the corporation appears to be protecting its culpable employees and agents. Thus, while cases will differ depending on the circumstances, a corporation's promise of support to culpable employees and agents either through the

> advancing of attorneys' fees,[*] through retaining the employees without sanction for their misconduct, or through providing information to the employees about the government's investigation pursuant to a joint defense agreement, may be considered by the prosecutor in weighing the extent and value of a corporation's cooperation. By the same token, the prosecutor should be wary of attempts to shield corporate officers and employees from liability by a willingness of the corporation to plead guilty. [Some states require corporations to pay the legal fees of officers under investigation prior to a formal determination of their guilt. Obviously, a corporation's compliance with governing law should not be considered a failure to cooperate.] Holder Memorandum, VI. B. (Memorandum's footnote in brackets at the asterisk above).

Although several academics and defense counsel expressed concern over the possible impact of the waiver feature of the Holder Memorandum,[61] a survey of United States Attorneys conducted in late 2002 indicated that waivers were rarely requested.[62]

Thompson Memorandum

On January 30, 2003, the Thompson Memorandum superseded the Holder Memorandum in a manner which hardly seemed designed to the meet the concerns of its critics. The Thompson Memorandum appeared to call for a more aggressive stance. The Thompson Memorandum was essentially a reissuance of its predecessor. Little of the text was new. That portion of the Memoranda devoted to the waiver of attorney-client and work product protections, and cooperation and voluntary disclosure in general—Part VI—was the same in both except for a new paragraph added in the Thompson Memorandum.[63] The addition said nothing about waivers per se, but made clear the risks that a corporation ran if it failed to be forthcoming early on or continued to support those officers or employees that prosecutors thought culpable:

> Another factor to be weighed by the prosecutor is whether the corporation, while purporting to cooperate, has engaged in conduct that impedes the investigation (whether or not rising to the level of criminal obstruction). Examples of such conduct include overly broad assertions of corporate representation of employees or former employees; inappropriate directions to employees or their counsel, such as directions not to cooperate openly and fully with the investigation including, for example, the direction

to decline to be interviewed; making presentations or submissions that contain misleading assertions or omissions; incomplete or delayed production of records; and failure to promptly disclose illegal conduct known to the corporation. Thompson Memorandum, VI. B.

Yet, this is one of the few amendments to the Holder Memorandum. To some, the whole scale adoption of language from the earlier Memorandum suggested a Justice Department perception that the problem with the Holder Memorandum was not its content, but rather its application. The Thompson Memorandum's description of the changes might be read to confirm this impression:

> The main focus of the revisions is increased emphasis on and scrutiny of the authenticity ofa corporation's cooperation. Too often business organizations, while purporting to cooperate with a Department investigation, in fact take steps to impede the quick and effective exposure of the complete scope of wrongdoing under investigation. The revisions make clear that such conduct should weigh in favor of a corporate prosecution. Thompson Memorandum, [Preamble].

Moreover, where the Holder Memorandum seemed to bespeak guidance, the Thompson Memorandum appeared to sound a command. The Holder Memorandum's preamble provided that, "These factors are, however, not outcome-determinative and are only guidelines. Federal prosecutors are not required to reference these factors in a particular case...." The remarks might have suggested that prosecutors enjoyed some significant degree of flexibility as to whether and how to apply the standards it announced. The Thompson Memorandum seemed to speak with a much more commanding tone; its introductory remarks stated that, "prosecutors and investigators in every matter involving business crimes *must* assess the merits of seeking the conviction of the business entity itself." Thompson Memorandum, [Preamble] (emphasis added).[64]

Comparable Policies Elsewhere

Nevertheless, the policies articulated in the Holder and Thompson Memoranda are similar to the enforcement policies announced by a substantial number of federal regulatory agencies that call for voluntary corporate disclosure of statutory or regulatory violations.[65] Some specifically mention the waiver of the attorney-client or work product protection,[66] while others seem to speak with sufficient generality to justify consideration on enforcement and sanction questions.[67]

Sentencing Guidelines

In May of 2004, the United States Sentencing Commission amended Commentary in the Sentencing Guidelines that some read as an endorsement of this new, more aggressive approach. The change explicitly described the circumstances under which a corporation's failure to waive could have sentencing consequences: "Waiver of attorney-client privilege and of work product protections is not a prerequisite to a reduction in culpability score under subdivisions (1) and (2) of subsection (g) unless such waiver is necessary in order to provide timely and thorough disclosure of all pertinent information known to the organization."[68]

Although apparently crafted at least in part to ease corporate anxiety,[69] it seemed to have the opposite effect.[70] The following August, the American Bar Association voted to recommend that the Commentary be changed to state that waiver should not be considered a sentencing factor.[71] The Commission instead removed from the Commentary the language quoted above that it had added in 2004.[72]

McCallum Memorandum

Then on October 21, 2005 came the McCallum Memorandum. It made no revision in the Thompson Memorandum, but briefly addressed the manner in which the Thompson Memorandum's policy on waiver was to be implemented. The various United States Attorneys were instructed to prepare written guidelines for supervisory approval of requests for corporate waivers.[73] The effort did little to assuage critics.[74]

Proposed Rules of Evidence

In January, 2006, the then Chairman of the House Judiciary Committee asked the Judicial Conference to consider a rule which would protect against inadvertent waiver of the attorney-client privilege, and which would permit protective court orders to limit the consequences of disclosure of privileged material during discovery, and selective waivers in the case of governmental investigations.[75] On May 15, 2006, the Federal Advisory Committee on Evidence opened for comment a proposed evidentiary rule amendment crafted, among other things, to resolve the split in the circuits and to afford corporations some relief in the form of selective waivers.[76] The proposed new Federal Rule of Evidence, proposed Rule 502, would have provided that disclosure of protected attorney-client or work product information to governmental investigators or regulators would not constitute a waiver of those protections with respect to third parties.[77]

The selective waiver feature of the rule, however, proved to be highly controversial and was dropped from the proposed rule the Judicial Conference recommended to the Congress.[78] Congress ultimately accepted the recommendation and enacted a rule with only inadvertent waiver and protective order components.[79]

Constitutional Concerns

In ther summer of 2006, a court in the Southern District of New York held that implementation of the Thompson Memorandum's policy with regard to a corporation's reimbursement of the attorneys' fees of its employees and pressure on them to make incriminating statements violated the Fifth Amendment substantive due process rights of the employees, their Fifth Amendment privilege against self-incrimination, as well as their Sixth Amendment right to the assistance of counsel.[80]

The case began with the criminal tax investigation of an accounting firm and its employees. After issuing subject letters to more than twenty of the firm's officers and employees, prosecutors met with the firm's attorneys.[81] At the meeting, the firm indicated that it intended to "clean house;" that it had already taken some personnel actions; that it meant to cooperate fully with the government's investigation; and that its objective was to avoid indictment of the firm and the fate of Arthur Andersen by acting so as to protect the firm and not the employees and officers targeted.[82] The firm indicated that it had been its practice to cover the litigation costs of its employees, but that it would not pay the fees of employees who refused to cooperate with the government's investigation or who invoked their Fifth Amendment privilege.[83] Prosecutors referred to the Thompson Memorandum and the Sentencing Guidelines and indicated they would take into account any instances where the firm was legally obligated to pay attorneys' fees.[84] They also indicated, however, that misconduct should not be rewarded and that prosecutors would examine "under a microscope" the payment of any fees that were not legally required.[85]

In consultation with prosecutors, the firm sent the subjects of the investigation form letters informing them that attorneys' fees would be capped at $400,000 and that fees would be cut off for any employee charged with criminal wrongdoing.[86] Thereafter, prosecutors advised the firm's attorney when one of the firm's employees proved uncooperative; the firm then advised the employees that they would be fired and their attorneys' fees cut off if they did not cooperate; and did so in cases of those employees who remained recalcitrant.[87] The firm then entered into a deferred prosecution agreement with prosecutors for the eventual dismissal of charges under which it agreed to waive indictment; pay a $456 million fine; accept restrictions on its practice; waive all privileges including but not limited to attorney-client and attorney work product; and provide the government with extensive cooperation in its investigation and prosecution of the firm's former officers and employees.[88]

The by-then indicted former officers and employees moved to have their indictments dismissed on constitutional grounds.[89] The court agreed that constitutional violations had occurred, but declined at least temporarily to dismiss the indictments under the understanding that the government had agreed that it would accept, without prejudice to the firm in its deferred prosecution agreement or otherwise, any fee arrangement that the firm should come to with its former officers and employees.[90] It subsequently dismissed the indictment against 13 of the defendants, but declined to do so with respect to three others who had left the firm sometime previously and therefore had not been the victims of the misconduct the court perceived.[91]

Substantive due Process

With regard to the constitutional provisions implicated in the *Stein* decision, the Fifth Amendment guarantees that "No person shall ... be deprived of life, liberty, or property, without due process of law," nor "be compelled in any criminal case to be a witness against himself," U.S.Const. Amend.

V. The Sixth Amendment promises that "[i]n all criminal prosecutions, the accused shall enjoy the right ... to have the Assistance of Counsel for his defence," U.S.Const. Amend. VI.

The Fifth Amendment due process clause and its twin in the Fourteenth Amendment contain both procedural and substantive components.[92] The courts have said that the substantive due process component of the due process clauses provides protection against the denial of any fundamental right to life, liberty, or property by "oppressive," "egregious or arbitrary" governmental action.[93] Given its sweeping potential breadth, the courts have been reluctant to recognize new claims to its safeguards.[94] They have noted that the component affords no protection against private deprivations,[95] imposes no affirmative duties upon government entities,[96] and protects only legally recognized entitlements not expectations or anticipated benefits.[97] Moreover, when "a particular Amendment provides an explicit textual source of constitutional protection against a particular sort of government behavior, that Amendment, not the more generalized notion of substantive due process, must be the guide for analyzing these claims."[98]

When substantive due process is found to include a particular fundamental right, infringement by government action may only survive if it is narrowly tailored to serve a compelling governmental interest.[99] Faced with the question of whether a particular type of government action is oppressive, egregious or arbitrary for substantive due process purposes, courts have often referred to the *Rochin* standard: government action cannot be said to violate substantive due process unless it first shocks the conscience of the court.[100]

The *Stein* court concluded that a criminal defendant has a substantive due process right "to obtain and use in order to prepare a defense resources lawfully available to him or her, free of knowing or reckless government interference."[101] It also found that the Thompson Memorandum and the pressure the prosecutors exerted upon the accounting firm to cut off the payment of attorneys' fees for the firm's former employees impinged upon the right.[102] While the court conceded that the government had a compelling interest in investigating and prosecuting crime and in preventing obstruction of those efforts, it felt the means chosen to serve its interests were insufficiently tailored to satisfy strict scrutiny:

> The first difficulty is that the Thompson Memorandum does not say that payment of legal fees may cut in favor of indictment *only if* it is used as a means to obstruct an investigation. Indeed, the text strongly suggests that advancement of defense[] costs weighs against an organization independent of whether there is any circling of the wagons... If the government means to take the payment of legal fees into account in making charging decisions only where the payments are part of an obstruction scheme—and thereby narrowly tailor its means to its ends—it would be easy enough to say so. But that is not what the Thompson Memorandum says.
>
> The concerns do not end here. The argument that payment of legal fees to employees and former employees is relevant to gauging the extent of a company's cooperation also is problematic. . . [I]t simply cannot be said that

> payment of legal fees for the benefit of employees and former employees necessarily or even usually is indicative of an unwillingness to cooperate fully. This is especially unlikely after employees have been indicted and fired, as is the situation here. *Id.* at 363-64 (emphasis in the original).

The *Stein* district court initially deferred dismissing the indictments in the hopes that an alternative remedy would develop.[103] When it took up the case again, it supplemented its earlier due process analysis with an assessment of whether the circumstances met the "shock" standard for substantive due process.[104] It concluded that the "government's actions with respect to legal fees were at least deliberately indifferent to the rights of the defendants and others. In all the circumstances, this behavior shocks the conscience in the constitutional sense whether prosecutors were merely deliberately indifferent to the KPMG Defendants' rights or acted more culpably."[105]

Self-Incrimination

The court resolved the self-incrimination issue in a separate decision following defendants' suppression motions.[106] Here the government was a bit more successful, for, although the court found a violation in some instances, it declined to do so in others.

As a general rule, statements secured under governmental threat of job termination are inadmissible in subsequent criminal proceedings.[107] During the course of the *Stein* case investigation, several employees had initially refused to talk to authorities. Prosecutors then brought the matter to the attention of the firm's attorneys and employees were told to cooperate or payment of their attorneys' fees would be discontinued and if still employed they would be fired.[108] In some cases, the coercion resulted in involuntary statements; in others, the employees made voluntary statements for reasons of their own notwithstanding the pressure.[109]

To the government's argument that no Fifth Amendment consequences flowed from the conduct of the firm, a private non-governmental actor, the court found the firm's conduct attributable to the government.[110] Yet in the end, only two of the nine challenged statements were suppressed.[111]

On appeal, the Second Circuit found it unnecessary to address either Fifth Amendment issue because of its treatment of the Assistance of Counsel issue.[112]

Assistance of Counsel

The Sixth Amendment assures the criminally accused the right to assistance of counsel "in all criminal prosecutions." It is said the right generally attaches once "prosecution has been commenced, that is, at or after the initiation of adversary judicial criminal proceedings—whether by way of formal charge, preliminary hearing, indictment, information, or arraignment."[113]

Once attached, the right includes the right to counsel of the defendant's choosing, subject to several limitations.[114] Among those limitations is the fact that an accused has no right to secure counsel of his choice using funds subject to confiscation, or as the Supreme Court stated, "[a] defendant has no Sixth Amendment right to spend another person's money for services rendered by an attorney, even if those funds are the only way that that defendant will be able to retain the attorney of his choice."[115]

The government contended that its conduct could not constitute a violation of the Sixth Amendment because (1) it had occurred before indictment and thus before the right to counsel had attached and (2) the employees had no Sixth Amendment right to pay for their counsel of choice with someone else's money.

Attachment was no obstacle, replied the court, when the motive or at least the clearly foreseeable result was to impede the employees criminal defense after they were indicted.[116] As for the Supreme Court's someone else's money comment, it referred to defendants using the government's money, money to which they had neither right nor expectation. Here, the court said the defendants had every reason to expect that the firm would have assumed their legal expenses, but for the government's intervention.[117]

In the eyes of the district court, the government's conduct so struck at the heart of the adversarial nature of the criminal justice system that it commanded redress without reference to proof of actual prejudice to its victims,[118] and warranted the rarely granted dismissal of the indictments.[119]

The court of appeals agreed.[120] It held (1) that "KPMG's adoption and enforcement of a policy under which it conditioned, capped and ultimately ceased advancing legal fees to defendants followed as direct consequence of the government's overwhelming influence;" (2) that "KPMG's conduct therefore amounted to state action;" (3) that " the government thus unjustifiably interfered with defendants' relationship with counsel and their ability to mount a defense in violation of the Sixth Amendment;" and (4) that "the government did not cure the violation."[121]

Legislative Activity in the 109th Congress

Both the House and Senate Judiciary Committees held hearings on the policy reflected in the Thompson Memorandum during the 109th Congress.[122] They heard contentions from some witnesses that:

- The policy represented a departure from past practices, since historically, Justice Department requests for waivers of corporate attorney-client and work product protection were unheard of.[123]
- "A culture of waiver has evolved in which government agencies believe it is reasonable and appropriate to them to expect a company under investigation to broadly waive."[124]
- Although characterized as "voluntary disclosures" or "waivers," in reality a company faced with a Justice Department request often has no alternative but to comply.[125]
- Company officials responsible for regulatory compliance are less likely to seek the advice of counsel if they believe those communications unprotected.[126]
- "[D]uring an investigation, if employees suspect that anything they say to their attorneys can be used against them, they won't say anything."[127]
- Even if a company should prove innocent of any criminal or regulatory wrongdoing, it may have lost the privilege against third party civil plaintiffs by virtue of its disclosure to the government.[128]

The Justice Department's perspective was a bit different. Its officials responded that:

- The Holder and Thompson Memoranda emerged in an environment of corporate scandal. Congress suggested, and the Department agreed, that enormous companies and their executives simply because of their wealth, position and influence should not be considered above the law, but should instead be held accountable if they engage in criminal conduct.[129]
- The Memoranda reflected an articulation of the principles that good prosecutors had long used in the context of a potential corporate prosecution.[130]
- The Department believed that waivers need not be, and had not been, routinely sought.[131]

- The Memoranda balance "the legitimate interests furthered by the privilege, and the societal benefits of rigorous enforcement of the laws supporting ethical standards of conduct."[132]
- Waiver was one, but only one, factor considered in the exercise of prosecutorial discretion.[133]
- The Department would support establishment of a selective waiver provision that would allow companies to continue to claim the attorney-client and work product protection against third parties notwithstanding disclosure to the government.[134]

In the final days of the 109th Congress, Senator Specter introduced S. 30 which, among other things, would have prohibited federal authorities from requesting a waiver of organizational attorney-client or work product protection or predicating the adverse exercise of prosecutorial discretion on the absence of such a waiver or the payment of attorneys' fees for their employees or officers.[135]

McNulty Memorandum

The McNulty Memorandum, announced December 12, 2006, superseded the Thompson and McCallum Memoranda.[136] While it incorporated a great deal of the substance of its predecessors, the McNulty Memorandum rewrote the principles and commentary that addressed corporate attorney-client and work product protection waivers as well as those covering the payment of employee litigation costs.

It dropped the specific reference to the waivers from the general statement of factors to be weighed when considering whether to charge a corporation.[137]

Earlier Memoranda stated that waiver was not an "absolute" requirement for the favorable exercise of prosecutorial discretion,[138] suggesting to some that it was a requirement under most circumstances. The McNulty Memorandum suggested that prosecutors' waiver requests were to be considered the exception rather than the rule:

> Prosecutors may only request waiver of attorney-client or work product protections when there is a legitimate need for the privileged information to fulfill their law enforcement obligations. A legitimate need for the information is not established by concluding it is merely desirable or convenient to obtain privileged information. The test requires a careful

balancing of important policy considerations underlying the attorney-client privilege and work product doctrine and the law enforcement needs of the government's investigation.

Whether there is a legitimate need depends upon:

(1) the likelihood and degree to which the privileged information will benefit the government's investigation;

(2) whether the information sought can be obtained in a timely and complete fashion by using alternative means that do not require waiver;

(3) the completeness of the voluntary disclosure already provided; and

(4) the collateral consequences to a corporation of a waiver. McNulty Memorandum, VII. B. 2.

Moreover, the McNulty Memorandum divided attorney-client and work product material into two categories. Category I consisted of factual information. Category II material was described in much the same manner as opinion work product material (It "might include the protection of attorney notes, memoranda or reports containing counsel's mental impressions, conclusions legal determinations reached as a result of an internal investigation, or legal advice given to corporation"), McNulty Memorandum, VII. B.2. The Memorandum cautioned prosecutors that only in rare circumstances should they seek the waiver of Category II material, id. A request for Category I had to be approved by the United States Attorney in consultation with the head of the Department's Criminal Division; a request for Category II information required prior approval of the Deputy Attorney General, id. A corporation's refusal to waive could not be considered in the exercise of prosecutorial discretion, id.

It also added an explicit provision concerning attorneys' fees, declaring that, "Prosecutors generally should not take into account whether a corporation is advancing attorneys' fees to employees or agents under investigation and indictment," id. at VII.B.3. On the other hand, it noted that, "In extremely rare cases, the advancement of attorneys' fees may be taken into account when the totality of the circumstances show that it was intended to impede a criminal investigation ... approval must be obtained from the Deputy Attorney General before prosecutors may consider this factor in their charging decisions," id. at VII.B.3. n.3.

Legislative Activity in the 110th Congress

The House and Senate Judiciary Committees held hearings during the 110th Congress which focused on the McNulty Memorandum and upon related legislative proposals.[139] Senator Specter introduced the Attorney-Client Privilege Protection Act of 2007 (S. 186) early in the 110th Congress,[140] which reappeared in revised form later in the Congress (S. 3217). S. 186 as introduced was identical to S. 30 (109th Cong.) that the Senator introduced at the end of the earlier Congress.[141] It was also identical to H.R. 3013 offered in the House by Representative Scott[142] and virtually identical to the version of that bill passed by the House.[143] In their final versions, they were much like their successors in the 111th Congress.

The testimony of some of the hearing witnesses and the views of some commentators applauded the changes in the McNulty Memorandum and questioned the justification for the legislative proposals on several grounds, e.g.:

- the McNulty Memorandum changes the tone of the policy, abandoning the aggressive implications of the Thompson Memorandum in favor of statements that confirm the Department's recognition and respect for the importance of the attorney-client privilege;[144]
- the Memorandum establishes a strict procedure for waiver requests and generally bars prosecutors from holding against a company its payment the legal expenses of an employee;[145]
- the Memorandum strikes the proper balance between the public's interest in vigorous investigation and prosecute white collar crime and fairness to corporations and their officers and employees;[146]
- experience since the issuance of the McNulty Memorandum refute the suggestion of widespread prosecutorial abuse; "legislative action is simply not needed;"[147]
- although the bills have no explicit enforcement mechanism and the courts are generally reluctant to impose sanctions in the absence of statutory authority, the bills' proposals are likely to bring forth a "cottage industry of prosecutorial abuse claims" that may deter the prosecution of worthy cases;[148]
- even if the Memorandum fosters an environment in which employees must waive their Fifth Amendment privilege or be fired, it results in no more than a situation in which the guilty suffer;[149]

- the legislative proposals will make prosecution of white collar crime more difficult because they reduce the incentive for corporate cooperation and thereby encourage "stonewalling."[150]

Others found the McNulty Memorandum troubling and applauded the legislative proposals for several reasons of their own, e.g.:

- the McNulty Memorandum will continue to result in routine compelled waiver of the attorney-client privilege and the work product protection;[151]
- the policy improvements contained in the McNulty Memorandum are not binding and lack an enforcement mechanism;[152]
- the Memorandum continues to allow prosecutors to encourage companies to fire employees who fail to waive their Fifth Amendment rights;[153]
- the Memorandum affords inadequate, partial attorney-client and attorney work product protection by assigning less stringent approval levels for waivers involving "factual" information which reveal client statements and attorney strategy;[154]
- the Memorandum addresses only Justice Department investigation and prosecution practices, whereas the legislative proposals reach the practices of other agencies as well;[155]
- the legislative proposals would not unduly impinge upon the prerogatives of federal prosecutors; to a limited extent, they bar interference with the attorney-client privilege, a mainstay of the Anglo-American system of justice since Elizabethan times and one whose presence has not heretofore been considered an unwarranted impediment to prosecution;[156]
- the proposals would "uphold the finest traditions of the DoJ by allowing it to strike harsh blows but fair ones in combating corporate crime."[157]

Senator Specter addressed some of these observations in S. 3217. S. 3217 expressly excluded from its protections certain terrorists organizations, illicit drug cartels, and crime-for-profit entities.[158] Where the earlier bar applied to federal criminal and civil matters and investigations alone, S. 3217 covered administrative adjudications and proceedings as well.[159] Where the earlier bills condemned governmental demands that an organization abandon its privileges, S. 3217 also removed any claim of those privileges from the permissible array of prosecutorial considerations.[160] Where the earlier bills permitted authorities to request information that they might reasonably consider beyond the scope of the privileges, S. 3217 also permitted them to seek information otherwise within the reach of a federal grand jury subpoena, privilege considerations notwithstanding, or to seek information whose privilege status was unknown to them.[161]

S. 3217 would have carried forward, with some modification, the subsections added to the House bill just before its passage there. The exception it afforded to instances, in which a statute "that *may* authorize" authorities to compel disclosure of privileged material, was revised to cover statutes "that authorize" compulsory access.[162]

Following House passage of H.R. 3013, then Deputy Attorney General Mark Filip issued a superseding memorandum accompanied by a revised chapter of the U.S. Attorneys Manual. The 110th Congress adjourned without further action of the proposals.

Filip Memorandum

The Filip Memorandum dates from August 28, 2008.[163] Following the pattern of earlier Memoranda, much of what appears in the U.S. Attorneys Manual is a verbatim recitation of the McNulty Memorandum. Some things, however, are new. The Filip Memorandum revisions "concern what measures a business entity must take to qualify for the long-recognized 'cooperation' mitigating factor, as well as how payment of attorneys' fees by a business organization for its officers or employees, or participation in a joint defense or similar agreement, will be considered in the prosecutive analysis."[164]

Thus, the Memorandum declares that "a corporation remains free to convey non-factual or 'core' attorney-client communications or work product—if and only if the corporation voluntarily chooses to do so—prosecutor should not ask for waivers and are directed not to do so."[165] Nevertheless, "cooperation is a potential mitigating factor, by which a corporation . . . can gain credit in a case that otherwise is appropriate for indictment and prosecution."[166] The entity's receipt of credit for its cooperation turns on its timely disclosure of information relating to the government's investigation, regardless of whether the entity acquired or maintains information under circumstances that entitle it to claim attorney-client or attorney work product protection.[167] Nor does a corporation's payment of its employees' attorneys' fees or its entry into a joint defense agreement preclude credit for cooperation.[168]

On the other hand, "[i]f the payment of attorney fees were used in a manner that would otherwise constitute criminal obstruction of justice—for example, if fees were advanced on the condition that an employee adhere to a version of the facts that the corporation and the employee knew to be false—these Principles would not (and could not) render inapplicable such criminal prohibitions."[169]

This represents a substantial modification of the previous standard in the McNulty Memorandum which explicitly permitted prosecutors to weigh negatively any number of specifically identified impediments—some well short of a criminal obstruction of justice.[170]

Legislative Activity in the 111th Congress

Early in the 111th Congress, Senator Specter introduced the Attorney-Client Privilege Protection Act of 2009 (S. 445), for himself and Senators Landrieu, Carper, Kerry, McCaskill, and Cochran. It is essentially the same as the later Specter proposal in the 110th Congress (S. 3217). Towards the end of the first session, Representative Scott (Va.) introduced a similarly styled Attorney-Client Privilege Protection Act of 2009 (H.R. 4326), for himself and Representatives Conyers, Smith (Tex.), Nadler, Delahunt, Coble, and Lungren. It is a replica of the bill which the House passed in the 110th Congress (H.R. 3013).

The two 111th Congress proposals are much the same, although with occasional differences. They espouse a common purpose: "to place on each agency clear and practical limits designed to serve the attorney-client privilege and work product protections available to an organization and preserve the constitutional rights and other legal protections available to employees of such an organization."[171]

They would define "attorney-client privilege" as currently understood under the federal law, that is as "the attorney-client privilege as governed by the principles of the common law, as they may be interpreted by the courts of the United States in the light of reason and experience, and the principles of article V of the Federal Rules of Evidence."[172] They would adopt an equally contemporaneous definition of "attorney work product," i.e., "materials prepared by, or at the direction of an attorney in anticipation of litigation, particularly any such materials that contain a mental impression, conclusion, opinion, or legal theory of that attorney."[173]

The Specter bill (S. 445) alone would insert a definition of "organization." The definition would foretell the scope of the bill, since the bill's commands speak to how federal prosecutors and investigators may deal with organizations. The bill's definition has two distinct components— what is an organization and what is not for purposes of the bill. It describes organizations as persons other than human beings and expressly includes state, local, and municipal governmental entities.[174] The absence of similar definition in the Scott bill (H.R. 4326) leaves open the question whether federal, state, local, and municipal entities fall within the scope of its provisions. The omission of federal and tribal governmental entities from the Specter bill's definition suggests that they would not be considered organizations for purposes of the bill.

The Specter bill (S. 445) would exclude from the definition of organization, drug cartels (continuing criminal enterprises (21 U.S.C. 848(c))); designated foreign terrorist organizations (18 U.S.C. 2339B(g)(6)); and entities charged under the RICO provisions.[175] The RICO exemption may raise questions. Common business organizations do not ordinarily include drug cartels or designated foreign terrorists organizations, but they are infrequently associated with RICO prosecutions. Federal racketeer influenced and corrupt organization (RICO) provisions proscribe, among other things, the patterned commission of two or more other federal or state offenses in order to conduct the affairs of an enterprise whose activities affect interstate or foreign commerce, 18 U.S.C. 1962(c). Depending upon the circumstances, an organization might either be an offender or the victimized intestate enterprise, 18 U.S.C. 1961(3), (4). Since the bill uses the phrase "entity charged," it might be thought to apply only to offending organizations and only after they are indicted. Such a reading, however, may be more narrow than its sponsors intend.

In somewhat different terms, the two bills would bar the Justice Department and other federal investigative, regulatory, or prosecutorial agencies from demanding that an organization:

- waive its attorney-client privilege or attorney work product protection;
- decline to pay the legal expenses of an employee;
- avoid joint defense, information sharing or common interest agreements with its employees;

- refrain from disclosing information concerning an investigation or enforcement action to employees; or
- terminate or discipline an employee for the employee's exercise of a legal right or prerogative with respect to a governmental inquiry.[176]

They would also preclude using such organizational activity as the basis in whole or in part for a civil or criminal charge against the organization.[177] Only the Specter bill (S. 445) would also prohibit the government from rewarding an organization for waiving its attorney-client privilege or work product protection.[178] The provision may be a response to criticism some commentators have leveled against the Filip Memorandum:

> The problem is rooted in the fact that indictments are fatal to major corporations. This means that from the beginning of the process, a corporation is compelled to follow the prosecutor's instructions on how to avoid indictment.
>
> Under the Filip revisions, like it was under the Thompson Memorandum, the way to avoid indictment is by cooperating with the government. Now, the government will not view negatively a corporation's refusal to give privileged information. It will, however, still give credit for that privileged information. Under the Filip revisions the compelling is done differently, almost passively—allowing the implied threat of indictment to do the work.[179]

Both bills would allow the government to request information it believes is beyond the scope of the attorney-client privilege or the attorney work product protection.[180] And they would not prevent an organization, on its own initiative, from sharing the results of an internal investigation with authorities, although the Specter bill (S. 445) would preclude the government from considering such a waiver positively.[181]

Each of the bills declares that its proposals are not intended to apply to situations when the government is statutorily authorized to demand a waiver.[182] It is not entirely clear what subsection 3014(e) intended to preserve when it referred to "any other federal statute that *may* authorize[s], in the course of an examination or inspection, an agent or attorney of the United States to require or compel the production of attorney-client privilege material."

Many federal statutes authorize the examination or inspection of corporate records and other materials.

Few, if any, federal statutes state in so many words that federal inspectors may examine otherwise privileged attorney-client or work product material. In fact, if privilege is mentioned at all, the statute is likely to preserve the privileged material against inspection.[183]

Use of the phrase in the Scott bill (H.R. 4326) that "any other federal statute that *may* authorize" may indicate that the authors of the subsection were referring to statutes which grant general authority that on a given occasion "may" extend to compelled access to privileged material. The absence of the word "may" in the Specter bill (S. 445)may be intended to limit the exception to instances of explicit statutory authority to demand.

The term "in the course of an examination or inspection" suggests that the exception likely would not extended to situations where the material was sought through an administrative or grand jury subpoena or through a civil investigative demand.

Finally, reference to "privileged" material narrows the category further and belies any intent to include material which on its face seems "privileged" but which because of the "crime or fraud" or some other exception cannot be classified as such. It is difficult to see what remains.

Finally, both bills would permit federal prosecutors, in determining whether to bring criminal charges against a corporation, to consider the fact the corporation had provided counsel for an employee, entered into a joint defense agreement with an employee, or shared information relating to investigation with an employee—but only when those activities are themselves federal crimes.[184]

Commentators who support the proposals argue that they are necessary (1) to overcome the "culture of waiver" produced by the Thompson Memorandum; (2) to establish consistent policy not only for the Department of Justice but for all federal investigative agencies; and (3) to provide stability and certainty that regularly shifting Justice Department policy statements cannot provide.[185]

Others contend that the proposals "would only frustrate the DOJ corporate charging policy, likely without altering the occurrence of waiver, but at the same time, rendering prosecutions needlessly complex."[186]

As of February 2010, neither House had held hearings on the proposals during the 111th Congress.

End Notes

[1] *New York Central R.R. v. United States*, 212 U.S. 481, 495-96 (1909); *United States v. Potter*, 463 F.3d 9, 25 (1st Cir. 2006)(internal quotation marks and citations omitted)("a corporation may be held liable for the criminal acts of its agents so long as those agents are acting within the scope of employment. The test is whether the agent is performing acts of the kind which he is authorized to perform and those acts are motivated—at least in part—by an intent to benefit the corporation.... The legal rules imputing criminal responsibility to corporations are built upon analogous rules for civil liability").

[2] *United States v. Wise*, 370 U.S. 405, 416 (1962); *United States v. Dotterweich*, 320 U.S. 277, 283 (1943).

[3] "*Arthur Andersen* taught that an indictment itself may be sufficiently damaging to close the doors of a public corporation," Boozang & Handler-Hutchinson, *"Monitoring" Corporate Corruption: DOJ's Use of Deferred Prosecution Agreements in Health Care*, 35 AMERICAN JOURNAL OF LAW AND MEDICINE 89, 89 (2009); Boese, McClain, & Hermandez-Stern, *Healthcare Behind Bars: The Use of Criminal Prosecutions in Forcing Corporate Compliance*, 3 JOURNAL OF HEATH & LIFE SCIENCE LAW 91, 106 (2009)("Not long after the allegations [against Enron] came to light, the government launched a sweeping probe focusing on Enron's accountant, Arthur Andersen. What brought down Arthur Anderson [sic] was not its audit work, but its response to a government subpoena. Arthur Andersen was accused of 'corruptly persuading its employees to destroy documents with an intent to impair their availability in a United States Securities and Exchange Commission (SEC) investigation ....' In 2002, Arthur Andersen was convicted of obstructing justice in the government's Enron investigation. By the time that verdict was reversed by the Supreme Court, Arthur Andersen was out of business").

[4] *Upjohn Co. v. United States*, 449 U.S. 383, 390 (1981)(citations omitted)("this Court has assumed that the privilege applies when the client is a corporation and the Government does not contest the general proposition"); cf., *Hickman v. Taylor*, 329 U.S. 495, 510-11 (1947).

[5] *United States v. Stein*, 435 F.Supp.2d 330, 356-72 (S.D.N.Y. 2006), *aff'd*, 541 F.3d 130 (2d Cir. 2008); *see also, United States v. Stein*, 495 F.Supp.2d 390 (S.D.N.Y. 2007).

[6] *White Collar Enforcement: Attorney-Client Privilege and Corporate Waivers: Hearing Before the Subcomm. on Crime, Terrorism, and Homeland Security of the House Comm. on the Judiciary*, 109th Cong., 2d Sess. (2006)(*House Hearings*); *The Thompson Memorandum's Effect on the Right to Counsel in Corporate Investigations: Hearing Before the Senate Committee on the Judiciary*, 109th Cong., 2d Sess. (2006)(*Senate Hearings); The McNulty Memorandum's Effect on the Right to Counsel in Corporate Investigations: Hearing Before the Subcomm. on Crime, Terrorism, and Homeland Security of the House Comm. on the Judiciary*, 110th Cong., 1st Sess. (2007)(House Hearings II); *Examining Approaches to Corporate Fraud Prosecutions and the Attorney-Client Privilege Under the McNulty Memorandum: Hearing Before the Senate Comm. on the Judiciary*, 110th Cong., 1st Sess. (2007)(Senate Hearings II).

[7] H.Rept. 110-445 (2007) (H.R. 3013 (110th Cong.)).

[8] 153 *Cong. Rec.* H13564 (daily ed. Nov. 13, 2007).

[9] U.S. Attorneys Manual, §9-28.000 et seq.

[10] F.R.Evid. 502, P.L. 110-322, 122 Stat. 3537 (2008). The new Rule protects against inadvertent waiver of the attorney-client privilege and the attorney work product doctrine and authorizes protective orders for case-specific waivers in both state and federal proceedings. As one point the proposed rule included a provision that allowed for selective waiver of the

attorney client privilege in the context of a governmental investigation, Rule 502. That feature had disappeared, however, by the time the Judicial Conference recommended the rule to the Congress, see discussion *infra* at 15-6.

[11] 1 BLACKSTONE, COMMENTARIES ON THE LAWS OF ENGLAND 464 (1765)(transliteration supplied)("A corporation cannot commit treason, or felony, or other crime, in it's corporate capacity: though it's members may, in their distinct individual capacities. Neither is it capable of suffering a traitor's, or felon's punishment, for it is not liable to corporal punishments, nor to attainder, forfeiture, or corruption of the blood").

[12] 1 U.S.C. 1; see e.g., *United States v. A & P Trucking Co.*, 358 U.S. 121, 124 (1958)(citing the Dictionary Act in support of the conclusion that a partnership might be held criminally liable for the improper transportation of explosives under a statute that applied to "whoever" breached its proscriptions).

[13] E.g., 18 U.S.C. 2 ("Whoever commits an offense against the United States ... is punishable as a principal"); 18 U.S.C. 371 ("If two or more persons conspire either to commit any offense against the United States, or to defraud the United States ... and one or more of such persons do any act to effect the object of the conspiracy, each shall be fined under this title"); 18 U.S.C. 661 ("Whoever, within the special maritime and territorial jurisdiction of the United States, takes and carries away, with intent to steal or purloin, any personal property of another shall be punished as follows.... ").

[14] E.g., 18 U.S.C. 1961(3)("As used in this chapter ... (3) 'person' includes any individual or entity capable of holding a legal or beneficial interest in property")(relating to racketeering offenses); 15 U.S.C. 7, 12(c) ("The word 'person', or 'persons' ... shall be deemed to include corporations and associations existing under or authorized by the laws of either the United States, laws of any of the Territories, the laws of any State, or the laws of any foreign country")(relating to the anti-trust laws).

[15] *United States v. Singh*, 518 F.3d 236, 249 (4th Cir. 2008); *United States v. Jorgensen*, 144 F.3d 550, 560 (8th Cir. 1998); *United States v. Investment Enterprises, Inc.*, 10 F.3d 263, 267 (5th Cir. 1994); *United States v. Paccione*, 949 F.2d 1183, 1200 (2d Cir. 1991); *United States v. Automated Medical Laboratories, Inc.*, 770 F.2d 399, 407 (4th Cir. 1985)("The term 'scope of employment' has been broadly defined to include acts on the corporation's behalf in performance of the agent's general line of work. To be acting within the scope of his employment, agent must be 'performing acts of the kind which he is authorized to perform, and those acts must be motivated—at least in part—by an intent to benefit the corporation'"), quoting, *United States v. Cincotta*, 689 F.2d 238, 241-42 (1st Cir. 1982).

[16] *United States v. Potter*, 463 F.3d 9, 25-6 (1st Cir. 2006)("The case law has rejected arguments that the corporation can avoid liability by adopting abstract rules. . . . Even a specific directive to an agent or employee or honest efforts to police such rules do not automatically free the company for the wrongful acts of agents. Thus the principal is held liable for acts done on his account by a general agent which are incidental or customarily a part of a transaction which the agent has been authorized to perform. And this is the case, even though it is established fact that the act was forbidden by the principal"); *United States v. Twentieth Century Fox*, 882 F.2d 656, 660 (2d Cir. 1989)("We agree with the District Court that Fox's compliance program, however extensive, does not immunize the corporation from liability when its employees, acting within the scope of their authority, fail to comply with the law and the consent decree. It is settled law that a corporation may be held criminally responsible for antitrust violations committed by its employees or agents acting within the scope of their authority"); *United States v. Portac, Inc.*, 869 F.2d 1288, 1293 (9th Cir. 1989).

[17] *United States v. Wise*, 370 U.S. 405, 416 (1962); *United States v. Dotterweich*, 320 U.S. 277, 283 (1943)(rejecting the contention that by establishing corporate liability Congress intended to exempt its culpable agents with the observation that, "It is not credible that Congress [in making it clear that the criminal prohibition applied to corporations] should by implication have exonerated what is probably a preponderant number of persons involved in acts of disobedience. . . ."); *United States v. Sain*, 141 F.3d 463, 475 (3d Cir. 1998).

[18] *Wayte v. United States*, 470 U.S. 598, 607 (1985); *United States v. LaBonte*, 520 U.S. 751, 762 (1997).

[19] *United States v. Stein*, 435 F.Supp. at 353-55, citing inter alia, 3A FLETCHER, CYCLOPEDIA OF THE LAW OF PRIVATE CORPORATIONS, §1344.10 (2002).

[20] *Id.*

[21] *Upjohn v. United States*, 449 U.S. 383, 389 (1981).

[22] *Swidler & Berlin v. United States*, 524 U.S. 399, 403 (1998); see also, *Upjohn v. United States*, 449 U.S. 383, 389 (1981); *Fisher v. United States*, 425 U.S. 391, 403 (1976); *Mohawk Industries, Inc. v. Carpenter*, 130 S.Ct. 599, 606 (2009).

[23] *Fisher v. United States*, 425 U.S. 391, 403 (1976); *In re Grand Jury*, 454 F.3d 511, 519 (6th Cir. 2006); *In re Grand Jury: Under Seal*, 415 F.3d 333, 338 n.3 (4th Cir. 2005)(The privilege applies if "(1) the asserted holder of the privilege is or sought to become a client; (2) the person to whom the communication was made (a) is a member of the bar of a court, or his subordinate and (b) in connection with this communication is acting as a lawyer; (3) the communication relates to a fact of which the attorney was informed (a) by his client (b) without the presence of strangers (c) for the purpose of securing primarily either (i) an opinion on law or (ii) legal services or (iii) assistance in some legal proceeding, and not (d) for the purpose of committing a crime or tort; and (4) the privilege as been (a) claimed and (b) not waived by the client"); *United States v. Bisanti*, 414 F.3d 168, 171 (1st Cir. 2005) ("The essential elements of the claim of attorney-client privilege are as follows: (1) Where legal advice of any kind is sought (2) from a professional legal adviser in his capacity as such, (3) the communications relating to that purpose, (4) made in confidence (5) by the client, (6) are at his insistance permanently protected (7) from disclosure by himself or by the legal adviser, (8) except the protection be waived "); *United States v. Ruehle*, 583 F.3d 600, 607 (9th Cir. 2009).

[24] *Commodity Futures Trading Comm'n v. Weintraub*, 471 U.S. 343, 348 (1985); *Upjohn Co. v. United States*, 449 U.S. 383, 389-90 (1981).

[25] *Upjohn Co. v. United States*, 449 U.S. at 390-97 (holding the privilege applicable to employee questionnaire responses as well as interview notes and memoranda collected during the course of an internal investigation conducted under the direction of the company's general counsel); *In re Allen*, 106 F.3d 582, 606-7 (4th Cir. 1997); *Admiral Insurance Co. v. U.S. District Court*, 881 F.2d 1486, 1492-493 (9th Cir. 1989).

[26] *Upjohn Co. v. United States*, 449 U.S. 383 (1981).

[27] *Id.* at 386.

[28] *Id.* at 386-87.

[29] *Id.* at 387.

[30] *Id.*

[31] *Id.* at 387-88.

[32] *Id.* at 388.

[33] *United States v. Upjohn Co.*, 600 F.2d 1223, 1225 (6th Cir. 1979)("Upjohn claims that the communications to counsel made by all of its employees including regular and middle management employees as well as top management, are privileged as confidential

communications between client and attorney. To the extent that the communications were made by officers and agents not responsible for directing Upjohn's actions in response to legal advice, we disagree for the simple reason that the communications were not the 'client's'").

[34] *Upjohn Co. v. United States*, 449 U.S. 383, 390-91 (1981)(internal citations omitted) ("Such a view, we think, overlooks the fact that the privilege exists to protect not only the giving of professional advice to those who can act on it but also the giving of information to the lawyer to enable him to give sound and informed advice. The first step in the resolution of any legal problem is ascertaining the factual background and sifting through the facts with an eye to the legally relevant.... In the case of the individual client the provider of information and the person who acts on the lawyer's advice are one and the same. In the corporate context, however, it will frequently be employees beyond the control group as defined by the court below—'officers and agents ... responsible for directing [the company's] actions in response to legal advice'—who will possess the information needed by the corporation's lawyers. Middle-level and indeed lower-level-employees can, by actions within the scope of their employment, embroil the corporation in serious legal difficulties, and it is only natural that these employees would have the relevant information needed by corporate counsel if he is adequately to advise the client with respect to such actual or potential difficulties").

[35] 449 U.S. at 392 (1981)(internal citations omitted) ("The control group test adopted by the court below thus frustrates the very purpose of the privilege by discouraging the communication of relevant information by employees of the client to attorneys seeking to render legal advice to the client corporation. The attorney's advice will also frequently be more significant to noncontrol group members than to those who officially sanction the advice, and the control group test makes it more difficult to convey full and frank legal advice to the employees who will put into effect the client corporation's policy").

[36] *Id.* ("The narrow scope given the attorney-client privilege by the court below not only makes it difficult for corporate attorneys to formulate sound advice when their client is faced with a specific legal problem but also threatens to limit the valuable efforts of corporate counsel to ensure their client's compliance with the law. In light of the vast and complicated array of regulatory legislation confronting the modern corporation, corporations, unlike most individuals, constantly go to lawyers to find out how to obey the law, particularly since compliance with the law in this area is hardly an instinctive matter").

[37] Otherwise "[c]ourts have been willing to allow corporate employees to assert a personal privilege with respect to conversations with corporate counsel, despite the fact that the privilege generally belongs to the corporation ... only by meeting certain requirements.... First, they must show they approached [counsel] for the purpose of seeking legal advice. Second, they must demonstrate that when they approached [counsel] they made it clear that they were seeking legal advice in their individual rather than in their representative capacities. Third, they must demonstrate that the [counsel] saw fit to communicate with them in their individual capacities, knowing that a possible conflict could arise. Fourth, they must prove that their conversations with [counsel] were confidential. And, fifth, they must show that the substance of their conversations with [counsel] did not concern matters within the company or the general affairs of the company," *United States v. International Brotherhood of Teamsters*, 119 F.3d 210, 215 (2d Cir. 1997); *see also*, *In re Grand Jury Subpoena*, 274 F.3d 563, 571 (1st Cir. 2001); *Grand Jury Proceedings v. United States*, 156 F.3d 1038, 1041 (10th Cir. 1998); *In re Bevell, Bresler & Schulman Asset Management Corp.*, 805 F.2d 120, 123-25 (3d Cir. 1986).

[38] *Commodity Futures Trading Comm'n v. Weintraub*, 471 U.S. at 348 (1985); *In re Grand Jury Proceedings*, 219 F.3d 175, 184-86 (1st Cir. 2001); *United States v. Dakota*, 197 F.3d 821, 825 (6th Cir. 1999); *Sprague v. Thorn Americas, Inc.*, 129 F.3d 1355, 1371 (10th Cir. 1997).

[39] *In re Qwest Communications International, Inc.*, 450 F.3d 1179, 1186-197 (10th Cir. 2006).

[40] *Diversified Industries v. Meredith*, 572 F.2d 596, 611 (8th Cir. 1977).

[41] *Permian Corp. v. United States*, 665 F.2d 1214, 1219-221 (D.C. Cir. 1981); *United States v. Massachusetts Institute of Technology*, 129 F.3d 681, 685-86 (1st Cir. 1997); *In re John Doe Corp.*, 675 F.2d 482, 489 (2d Cir. 1982); *Westinghouse Electric Corp. v. Republic of the Philippines*, 951 F.2d 1414, 1425-426 (3d Cir. 1991); *In re Martin Marietta Corp.*, 856 F.2d 619, 623-24 (4th Cir. 1988); *In re Qwest Communications International Inc.*, 450 F.3d 1179, 1200 (10th Cir. 2006).

[42] *Hanson v. United States Agency for International Development*, 372 F.3d 286, 292 (4th Cir. 2004); see also, *United States v. Doe*, 429 F.3d 450, 453 (3d Cir. 2005).

[43] *United States v. Almeida*, 341 F.3d 1318, 1324 (11th Cir. 2003); see also, *United States v. Austin*, 416 F.3d 1016, 1021 (9th Cir. 2005); *In re Grand Jury Subpoena*, 274 F.3d 563, 574-75 (1st Cir. 2001).

[44] *In re Grand Jury Subpoenas*, 902 F.2d 244, 248(4th Cir. 1990); *John Morrell & Co. v. Local Union 304A*, 913 F.2d 544, 555 (8th Cir. 1990); *In re Auclair*, 961 F.2d 65, 70-1 (5th Cir. 1992); but see, *In re Grand Jury Subpoena*, 274 F.3d 563, 572-73 (1st Cir. 2001)("a party is always free to disclose his own communications ... a corporation may unilaterally waive the attorney-client privilege with respect to any communications made by a corporate officer in his corporate capacity, notwithstanding the existence of an individual attorney-client relationship between him and the corporation's counsel").

[45] 329 U.S. 495 (1947).

[46] F.R.Civ.P. 26; *Upjohn v. United States*, 449 U.S. 383, 396 (1981); *Regional Airport Authority v. LFG, LLC*, 460 F.3d 697, 713 (6th Cir. 2006); *In re Qwest Communications International, Inc.*, 450 F.3d 1179, 1186 (10th Cir. 2006).

[47] F.R.Crim.P. 16; *United States v. Nobles*, 422 U.S. 225, 236-39 (1975).

[48] *United States v. Nobles*, 422 U.S. at 238-39; see also, *Hickman v. Taylor*, 329 U.S. at 511-14 ("Proper preparation of a client's case demands that he assemble information, sift what he considers to be the relevant from the irrelevant facts, prepare his legal theories and plan his strategy without undue and needless interference.... Were such materials open to opposing counsel on mere demand, much of what is now put down in writing would remain unwritten ... Inefficiency, unfairness and sharp practices would inevitably develop in the giving of legal advice and in the preparation of cases for trial").

[49] *United States v. Nobles*, 422 U.S. at 239.

[50] This is distinguished from "non-opinion" or "fact" work product which consists of all other material gathered or produced by or at the direction of an attorney in anticipation of litigation.

[51] *In re Martin Marietta Corp.*, 856 F.2d 619, 625-26 (4th Cir. 1988); *In re Echostar Communications Corp.*, 448 F.3d 1294, 1301-305 (Fed. Cir. 2006).

[52] *Westinghouse Electric Corp. v. Republic of the Philippines*, 951 F.2d 1414, 1429 (3d Cir. 1991).

[53] *In re Qwest Communications International, Inc.*, 450 F.3d 1179, 1192, 1194 (10th Cir. 2006)(refusing to acknowledge survival of the protection under the facts before it rather than as a general rule)("we conclude the record in this case is not sufficient to justify adoption of a selective waiver doctrine as an exception to the general rules of waiver upon disclosure of protected material.... In short, Qwest's confidentiality agreements do not

support adoption of selective waiver"); *In re Columbia/HCA Healthcare Corp. Billing Practices Litigation*, 293 F.3d 289, 307 (6th Cir. 2002)(emphasis added)(footnote 30 of the court's opinion in brackets)("These and other reasons persuade us that the standard for waiving the work-product doctrine should be no more stringent than the standard for waiving the attorney-client privilege—once the privilege is waived, waiver is complete and final. [*This is especially true as to 'fact' work product....*"]; *United States v. Massachusetts Institute of Technology*, 129 F.3d 681, 688 (1st Cir. 1997)(holding the protection waived under the facts before it but noting that the decision does not address whether "opinion" work product protection might survive disclosure to the government); *In re Steinhardt Partners*, 9 F.3d 230, 235-36 (2d Cir. 1993)(holding the party waived work product production by voluntarily turning material over to the SEC, but "declin[ing] to adopt a *per se* rule that all voluntary disclosures to the government waive work product protection"); *In re Chrysler Motors Corp.*, 860 F.2d 844, 846 (8th Cir. 1989)(holding the party waived work product protection by voluntary disclosure, but noting that the material did not include "opinion" work product "which enjoys a very near absolute immunity and can be discovered only in very rare and extraordinary circumstances"); *In re Subpoena Duces Tecum*, 738 F.2d 1367, 1375 (D.C. Cir. 1984)(emphasis added)("we cannot see how the developing procedure of corporations to employ independent outside counsel to investigate and advise them would be thwarted by telling a corporation that it cannot disclose the resulting reports to the SEC if it wishes to maintain their confidentiality. The same choice is open under the work product privilege. *Or the company can insist on a promise of confidentiality before disclosure to the SEC*").

[54] "Bringing Criminal Charges Against Corporations," Memorandum from the Deputy Attorney General, to All Component Heads and United States Attorneys, dated as signed on June 16, 1999, (Holder Memorandum), 66 *BNA Criminal Law Reporter* 189 (December 8, 1999).

[55] "Principles of Federal Prosecution of Business Organizations," Memorandum from Larry D. Thompson, Deputy Attorney General, to Heads of Department Components and United States Attorneys, dated January 20, 2003, (Thompson Memorandum), available at http://www.justice.gov/dag/cftf/corporate_guidelines.htm.

[56] "Principles of Federal Prosecution of Business Organizations," Memorandum from Paul J. McNulty, Deputy Attorney General, to Heads of Department Components and United States Attorneys, undated, (McNulty Memorandum), available at http://www.justice.gov/dag /speech/2006/mcnulty_memo.pdf.

[57] "Principles of Federal Prosecution of Business Organizations," Memorandum from Mark Filip, Deputy Attorney General to Heads of Department Components [and] United States Attorneys, dated August 28, 2008 (Filip Memorandum)(with U.S. Attorneys Manual, Title 9, Chapter 9-28.000 attached), available at http://www.justice.gov/dag/readingroom/dag-memo-08282008.pdf.

[58] "Waiver of Corporate Attorney-Client and Work Product Protection," Memorandum from Robert D. McCallum, Jr., Acting Deputy Attorney General, to Heads of Department Components and United States Attorneys, dated October 21, 2005, (McCallum Memorandum) (we have been unable to locate on the Justice Department's website the McCallum Memorandum which previously appeared in the Justice Department's Criminal Resource Manual), available on Westlaw as either SL031 ALI_ABA 1299 or 1571 PLI/Corp 705; *see also*, 78 *BNA Criminal Law Reporter* 183.

[59] Holder Memorandum, II. Charging Corporations—Factors To Be Considered, A. General Principle. The Sentencing Commission had declared similar considerations appropriate organizational sentencing factors, *United States Sentencing Commission Guideline Manual*,

U.S.S.G. §8C2.5 (1991 ed.), 56 *Fed.Reg.* 22791-792 (May 16, 1991)(indicating that a convicted organization's culpability score should be determined by weighing a corporation's involvement in or tolerance of criminal activity; its prior history; any evidence of its efforts to obstruct justice; the existence of a organizational compliance program; and the extent to which the organization reported the criminal activity, cooperated with the investigation, and accepted responsibility).

[60] Holder Memorandum, VI.A.

[61] Zornow & Krakaur, *On the Brink of a Brave New World: The Death of Privilege in Corporate Criminal Investigations*, 37 AMERICAN CRIMINAL LAW REVIEW 147, 156 (2000)("Thus unfettered, federal prosecutors are authorized by Justice Department policy to rend the fabric of confidential communications ranging from those that occurred around the time of the conduct at issue to those that occurred during and in connection with the criminal investigation itself. And once these privileges have been waived, they will likely become fair game for plaintiffs in civil suits"); Cole, *Revoking Our Privileges: Federal Law Enforcement's Multi-Front Assault on the Attorney-Client Privilege (and Why It Is Misguided)*, 48 VILLANOVA LAW REVIEW 469, 543 (2003)("These statements in the Holder Memorandum go quite far toward effectively forcing a corporation to waive privilege protections if it hopes to obtain favorable charging treatment at the hands of DOJ prosecutors. In complex corporate criminal cases federal prosecutors have enormous prosecutorial discretion to decide the nature and number of charges, if any, that they will bring against the responsible corporate entity and culpable individuals. Moreover, the manner in which that prosecutorial discretion is exercised is not subject to legal challenges or judicial review. This combination of broad discretion and limited accountability presents the potential for misguided policy decisions and, in the worst cases, even abuses of governmental power"); *The Erosion of the Attorney-Client Privilege and Work Product Doctrine in Federal Criminal Investigations: A Report Prepared by the American College of Trial Lawyers*, 41 DUQUESNE LAW REVIEW 307 (2003)("The Justice Department's policy, as expressed in the Holder Memo Standards, is to obtain waivers of the corporate attorney-client and work-product privilege where, in the government's view these protections might keep information relevant to a criminal investigation from discovery. Indeed, there is no pretense that the values underlying these privileges are to be sacrificed for any reason other than to make the prosecution's job easier").

[62] Buchanan, *Effective Cooperation by Business Organizations and. the Impact of Privilege Waivers*, 39 WAKE FOREST LAW REVIEW 587, 597-98 (2004); United States Sentencing Commission, *Report of the Ad Hoc Advisory Group on the Organizational Sentencing Guidelines* 98-9 (October 7, 2003).

[63] See Berry, *Revised Principles of Federal Prosecutions of Business Organizations: An Overview*, 51 UNITED STATES ATTORNEYS' BULLETIN 8 (November 2003)("One significant 'non-revision' of the Holder memo is noteworthy. Amidst controversy, no change in the use of waivers of the attorney-client and work protect protections has been included in the Thompson memo").

[64] Cf., *United States v. Stein*, 435 F.Supp.2d 330, 338 (S.D.N.Y. 2006)("Unlike its predecessor, however, the Thompson Memorandum is binding on all federal prosecutors").

[65] For a description of several of these see, Wray & Hur, *Corporate Criminal Prosecution in a Post-Enron World: The Thompson Memo in Theory and Practice*, 43 AMERICAN CRIMINAL LAW REVIEW 1095, 1118-135 (2006).

[66] E.g., U.S. Commodity Futures Trading Commission, Division of Enforcement, *Enforcement Advisory: Cooperation Factors in Enforcement Division Sanction Recommendations* ("The

three areas of a company's conduct that bear on the Division's decision-making about sanctions recommendations include the following ... II. Quality of the Company's Efforts in Cooperating with the Division and Managing the Aftermath of the Misconduct... 3. Did the company willing: a. waive corporate attorney-client and work product protection and other corporate documents? b. waive corporate attorney-client privilege for employee testimony? ..."); Securities Exchange Commission, *Report of Investigation Pursuant to Section 21(a) of the Securities Exchange Act of 1934 and Commission Statement on the Relationship of Cooperation to Agency Enforcement Decisions*, Release No. 44969 (October 23, 2001) (Seaboard Report)("In brief form, we set forth below some of the criteria we will consider in determining whether, and how much, to credit self-policing, self-reporting, remediation and cooperation—from the extraordinary step of taking no enforcement action to bringing reduced charges, seeking lighter sanctions, or including mitigating language in documents we use to announce and resolve enforcement actions.... In some cases, the desire to provide information to the Commission staff may cause companies to consider choosing not to assert the attorney-client privilege, the work product protection and other privileges, protections, and exemptions with respect to the Commission... Did the company promptly make available to our staff the results of its review... did the company identify possible violative conduct and evidence with sufficient precision to facilitate prompt enforcement actions ... In this regard, the Commission does not view a company's waiver of a privilege as an end in itself, but only as a means (where necessary) to provide relevant and sometimes critical information to the Commission").

[67] E.g., Federal Energy Regulatory Commission, *Policy Statement on Enforcement*, 113 FERC ¶ 61,068 (October 20, 2005)("the Commission will consider these factors even for entities that did not self-report violations, provided that cooperation was provided once the violation was uncovered. > Did the company volunteer to provide internal investigation or audit reports relating to the misconduct ... > Did the company ... actively encourage [its] employees to provide the Commission with complete ... information?"); Federal Financial Institutions Examination Council, *Assessment of Civil Money Penalties*, 63 *Fed.Reg.* 30226, 30227 (June 3, 1998)("In determining the amount and the appropriateness of initiating a civil money penalty assessment proceeding ... the agencies have identified the following factors as relevant... (4) The failure to cooperate with the agency in effecting early resolution of the problem; (5) Evidence of concealment of the violation, practice, or breach of fiduciary duty or, alternatively, voluntary disclosure of the violation, practice or breach of fiduciary duty").

[68] 69 *Fed.Reg.* 29021 (May 19, 2004); *United States Sentencing Commission Guidelines Manual*, U.S.S.C. §8C2.5, Commentary Note 12 (2004 ed.).

[69] United States Sentencing Commission, *Reason for the Amendment*, 69 *Fed.Reg.* 29024 (May 19, 2004).

[70] Brown, *Reconsidering the Corporate Attorney-Client Privilege: A Response to the Compelled-Voluntary Waiver Paradox*, 34 HOFSTRA LAW REVIEW 897, 937 (2006) ("Whatever faint distinctions existed between the two Memos, the ultimate result appears to be the same, at least from the perspective of the corporate bar, namely, routine demands by DOJ for waiver, which corporations feel compelled to provide... The amendment to the U.S. Sentencing Guidelines, suggesting that waiver could be a prerequisite to the reduction of a corporation's culpability score under certain circumstances, added further credence to this perception"); McLucas, Shapiro & Song, *The Decline of the Attorney-Client Privilege in the Corporate Setting*, 96 JOURNAL OF CRIMINAL LAW AND CRIMINOLOGY 621, 634 (2006)("The U.S. Sentencing Commission has validated the DOJ view of waiver of the

attorney-client privilege by recent amendments to the Organizational Sentencing Guidelines. In particular, recently amended Commentary to §8C2.5 ... [in which] the exception is likely to swallow the rule; prosecutors will make routine requests for waivers and organizations will be forced to routinely grant them").

[71] American Bar Association Task Force on Attorney-Client Privilege, *Report to the House of Delegates* 4 n.4 (2006)

[72] 71 *Fed.Reg.* 28073 (May 15, 2006)("The Commission added this sentence to address some concerns regarding the relationship between waivers and §8C2.5(g), and at the time stated that '[t]he Commission expects that such waivers will be required on a limited basis.' Subsequently, the Commission received public comment and heard testimony at public hearings ... that the sentence at issue could be misinterpreted to encourage waivers").

[73] "To ensure that federal prosecutors exercise appropriate prosecutorial discretion under the principles of the Thompson Memorandum, some United States Attorneys have established review processes for waiver requests that require federal prosecutors to obtain approval from the United States Attorney or other supervisor before seeking a waiver of the attorney-client privilege or work product protection. Consistent with this best practice, you are directed to establish a written waiver review process of your district or component. The United States Attorneys' Manual will be amended to reflect this policy. Such waiver review processes may vary from district to district (or component to component), so that each United States Attorney or component head retains the prosecutorial discretion necessary, consistent with their circumstances, to seek timely, complete, and accurate information from business organizations," McCallum Memorandum.

[74] McLucas, Shapiro & Song, *The Decline of the Attorney-Client Privilege in the Corporate Setting*, 96 JOURNAL OF CRIMINAL LAW AND CRIMINOLOGY 621, 633 (2006)("The McCallum Memo ensures that each U.S. Attorney across the country will be ready to strike with a demand for a privilege waiver. Significantly, it does not require consistency or predictability across offices in making these demands—an issue that is particularly troublesome for corporations doing business in a global marketplace").

[75] Letter from Chairman F. James Sensenbrenner, Jr. to Director Leonidas Ralph Mecham, Administrative Office of the United States Courts, dated January 23, 2006, available on October 11, 2008 at http://www.uscourts.gov/rules/2006-01- 23-Sensenbrenner.pdf.

[76] Memorandum from the Honorable Jerry E. Smith, Chair of the Advisory Committee on Evidence Rules to the Honorable David F. Levi, Chair of the Standing Committee on Rules of Practice and Procedure, relating to a Report of the Advisory Committee on Evidence Rules and dated May 15, 2006, available on October 11, 2008 at http://www.uscorts.gov/rules/Report/ev05_2006.pdf.

[77] "In a federal or state proceeding, a disclosure of a communication or information covered by the attorney-client privilege or work product protection—when made to a federal public office or agency in the exercise of its regulatory, investigative, or enforcement authority—does not operate as a waiver of the privilege or protection in favor of nongovernmental persons or entities. The effect of disclosure to a state or local government agency, with respect to nongovernmental persons or entities is governed by applicable state law. Nothing in this rule limits or expands the authority of a government agency to disclose communications or information to other government agencies or as otherwise authorized or required by law," proposed F.R.Evid. 502(c).

[78] Letters from Judge Lee H. Rosenthal, Chair of the Comm. On Rules and Procedure of the Judicial Conference of the United States to Senators Patrick J. Leahy and Arlen Specter as well as Representatives John Conyers, Jr., and Lamar Smith, each dated January 26, 2007,

at 6, available on October 11, 2008 at http://www.uscourts.gov/rules/Hill_Letter_re_Ev_502.pdf.

[79] F.R.Evid. 502, P.L. 110-322, 122 Stat. 3537 (2008). See also, S.Rept. 110-264 (2008).

[80] *United States v. Stein*, 435 F.Supp.2d 330, 356-72 (S.D.N.Y. 2006); *United States v. Stein*, 440 F.Supp.2d 315, 337- 38 (S.D.N.Y. 2006).

[81] *United States v. Stein*, 435 F.Supp.2d at 341.

[82] *Id. See also*, *United States v. Stein*, 440 F.Supp.2d 315, 337 (S.D.N.Y. 2006)("Many companies faced with allegations of wrongdoing are under intense pressure to avoid indictment, as an indictment—especially of a financial services firm—threatens to destroy the business regardless of whether the firm ultimately is convicted or acquitted. That is precisely what happened to Arthur Andersen & Co., one of the world's largest accounting firms, which collapsed almost immediately after it was indicted—and the Supreme Court's eventual reversal of its conviction did not undo the damage. So any entity facing such catastrophic consequences must do whatever it can to avoid indictment").

[83] *Id.* at 342.

[84] *Id.* at 342-43.

[85] *Id.* at 344.

[86] *Id.* at 345-46.

[87] *Id.* at 347.

[88] *Id.* at 349.

[89] *Id.* at 350.

[90] *Id.* at 382.

[91] *United States v. Stein*, 495 F.Supp. 390, 425-28 (S.D.N.Y. 2007).

[92] *Reno v. Flores*, 507 U.S. 292, 301 (1993)("Respondents' 'substantive due process' claim relies upon our line of cases which interprets the Fifth and Fourteenth Amendments' guarantee of 'due process of law' to include a substantive component, which forbids the government to infringe certain fundamental liberty interests at all, no matter what process is provided, unless the infringement is narrowly tailored to serve a compelling state interest'); see also, *Washington v. Glucksberg*, 521 U.S. 702, 719 (1997); *Collins v. Harker Heights*, 503 U.S. 115, 1992 (1992).

[93] *Cuyahoga Falls v. Buckeye Community Hope Foundation,* 538 U.S. 188, 198 (2003); *Sacramento v. Lewis*, 523 U.S. 833, 846 (1998); *Collins v. Harker Heights*, 503 U.S. 115, 126 (1992); *DeShaney v. Winnebago County Dept. of Social Services*, 489 U.S. 189, 196 (1989).

[94] *Washington v. Glucksberg*, 521 U.S. 702, 720 (1997) ("we have always been reluctant to expand the concept of substantive due process because guideposts for responsible decisionmaking in this unchartered area are scarce and open-ended. By extending constitutional protection to an asserted right or liberty interest, we, to a greatest extent, place the matter outside the area of public debate and legislative action. We must therefore exercise the utmost care whenever we are asked to break new ground in this field, lest the liberty protected by the Due Process Clause be subtly transformed into the policy preferences of the Members of this Court"); see also, *Collins v. Harker Heights*, 503 U.S. 115, 125 (1992).

[95] *Castle Rock v. Gonzales*, 545 U.S. 748, 755 (2005); *DeShaney v. Winnebago Country Dept. of Social Services*, 489 U.S. 189, 195 (1989).

[96] *Collins v. Harker Heights*, 503 U.S. 115, 126 (1992).

[97] *Castle Rock v. Gonzales*, 545 U.S. at 756; *Board of Regents v. Roth*, 408 U.S. 564, 577 (1972).

98 *Sacramento v. Lewis*, 523 U.S. 833, 842 (1998); see also, *Albright v. Oliver*, 510 U.S. 266, 273 (1994).

99 *Reno v. Flores*, 507 U.S. at 302; *Collins v. Harker Heights*, 503 U.S. at 125.

100 *Chavez v. Martinez*, 538 F.3d 760, 774 (2003)("Convictions based on evidence obtained by methods that are so brutal and so offensive to human dignity that they shock the conscience violate the Due Process Clause. *Rochin v. California*, 342 U.S. 165, 172, 174 (1952)"); *Sacramento v. Lewis*, 523 U.S. 833, 847 n.8 (1998); *Collins v. Harker Heights*, 503 U.S. 115, 128 (1992); *Ellis v. Ogden City*, 589 F.3d 1099, 1101 (10th Cir. 2009); *Chambers v. School District of Philadelphia*, 587 F.3d 176, 190 (3d Cir. 2009); *Okin v. Village of Cornwall-on-Hudson Police Department*, 577 F.3d 415, 431 (2d Cir. 2009); *Maldonado v. Fontanes*, 568 F.3d 263, 272 (1st Cir. 2009); *Corales v. Bennett*, 567 F.3d 554, 568 (9th Cir. 2009); *Wolf v. Fauquier County Board of Supervisors*, 555 F.3d 311, 323 (4th Cir. 2009); *United States v. Rutherford*, 555 F.3d 190, 195 (6th Cir. 2009); *Alvear-Velez v. Mukasey*, 540 F.3d 672, 682 n.6 (7th Cir. 2008); *Marco Outdoor Advertising, Inc. v. Regional Transit Authority*, 489 F.3d 669, 672 n3 (5th Cir. 20078); *Estate of Phillips v. District of Columbia*, 455 F.3d 397, 403 (D.C. Cir. 2006).

101 *United States v. Stein*, 435 F.Supp.2d at 361-62.

102 *Id.* at 362 (The court calculated that "even a minimal defense of this case could well cost $500,000 to $1 million, if not significantly more").

103 *United States v. Stein*, 495 F.Supp.2d 390, 394 (S.D.N.Y. 2007).

104 *Id.* at 412-15.

105 *Id.* at 415. The circumstances included the fact from the court's perspective the United States Attorney's Office had been "'economical with the truth' in its effort to avoid an evidentiary hearing on the defendants' motion with respect to the fee issues," *id.* at 410. Perhaps more telling, however, was the impact of reduced resources available to defendants in a case that involved more than 22 million pages of evidentiary material and complex legal issues that had resulting in twenty-four separate court opinions by the time the indictments were dismissed, *id.* at 417-18.

106 *United States v. Stein*, 440 F.Supp.2d 315 (S.D.N.Y. 2006).

107 *Garrity v. New Jersey*, 385 U.S. 493, 496-500 (1967); *United States v. Moten*, 551 F.3d 763, 766 (8th Cir. 2008); *United States v. Waldon*, 363 F.3d 1103, 1112 (11th Cir. 2004).

108 *United States v. Stein*, 440 F.Supp.2d at 330-33.

109 *Id.*

110 *Id.* at 337 ("the government, both through the Thompson Memorandum and the actions of the [United States Attorney's Office], quite deliberately coerced, and in any case significantly encouraged, [the firm] to pressure its employees to surrender their Fifth Amendment rights. There is a clear nexus between the government and specific conduct of which the Moving Defendants complain").

111 *Id.* at 338.

112 *United States v. Stein*, 541 F.3d 130, 136, 136 n.2 (2d Cir. 2008)(footnote 2 of the court's opinion in brackets) ("[In a separate summary order filed today, we dismiss as moot the government's appeal from the order of the district court suppressing [on grounds of self-incrimination] proffer statements made by Defendants-Appellees Smith and Watson.] In light of this disposition, we do not reach the district court's Fifth Amendment [due process] ruling").

113 *Texas v. Cobb*, 532 U.S. 162, 166 (2001); see also, *McNeil v. Wisconsin*, 501 U.S. 171, 175 (1991); *United States v. Mills*, 412 F.3d 325, 328 (2d Cir. 2005).

[114] *Wheat v. United States*, 486 U.S. 153, 159 (1988)("The Sixth Amendment right to choose one's own counsel is circumscribed in several important respects. Regardless of his persuasive powers, an advocate who is not a member of the bar may not represent clients (other than himself) in court. Similarly, a defendant may not insist on representation by an attorney he cannot afford or who for other reasons declines to represent the defendant. Nor may a defendant insist on the counsel of an attorney who has a previous or ongoing relationship with an opposing party, even when the opposing party is the government"); see also, *United States v. Gonzalez-Lopez*, 548 U.S. 140, 144 (2006).

[115] *Caplin & Drysdale v. United States*, 491 U.S. 617, 626 (1989); see also, *United States v. Monsanto*, 491 U.S. 600, 614-615 (1989).

[116] *United States v. Stein*, 435 F.Supp.2d at 366.

[117] *Id.* at 367 ("Thus, both the expectation and any benefits that would have flowed from that expectation—the legal fees at issue now—were, in every material sense, their property not that of a third party").

[118] *Id.* at 368-73 (noting the similarity to *Gonzalez-Lopez*, and observing that the "Thompson Memorandum discourages and, as a practical matter, often prevents companies from providing employees and former employees with the financial means to exercise their constitutional rights to defend themselves. This is so even where companies obstruct nothing and, to the contrary, do everything within their power to make a clean breast of the facts to the government and to take responsibility for any offenses they may have committed. It undermines the proper functioning of the adversary process that the constitution adopted as a mode of determining guilt or innocence in criminal cases. The actions of prosecutors who implement it can make matters even worse, as occurred here"). *See also*, *United States v. Stein*, 495 F.Supp.2d 390, 426-27 (S.D.N.Y. 2007)("The Department of Justice, in promulgating the aspects of the Thompson Memorandum here at issue, and the USAO in the respects discussed above and in Stein I, deliberately or callously prevented many of these defendants from obtaining funds for their defense that they lawfully would have had absent the government's interference. They thereby foreclosed these defendants from presenting the defense they wished to present, and in some cases, even deprived them of counsel of their choice. This is intolerable in a society that holds itself out to the world as a paragon of justice").

[119] *Id.* at 427.

[120] *United States v. Stein*, 541 F.3d 130, 136 (2d Cir. 2008).

[121] *Id.*

[122] *White Collar Enforcement: Attorney-Client Privilege and Corporate Waivers: Hearing Before the Subcomm. on Crime, Terrorism, and Homeland Security of the House Comm. on the Judiciary*, 109th Cong., 2d Sess. (2006)(*House Hearings)*; *The Thompson Memorandum's Effect on the Right to Counsel in Corporate Investigations: Hearing Before the Senate Committee on the Judiciary*, 109th Cong., 2d Sess. (2006)(*Senate Hearings)*.

[123] *House Hearings* 13-4 (testimony of former U.S. Attorney General Thornburgh).

[124] *House Hearings* 13 (testimony of former U.S. Attorney General Thornburgh).

[125] *House Hearings* 17 (testimony of U.S. Chamber of Commerce, President and CEO Thomas J. Donohue) ("A company that refuses to waive its privilege risks being labeled as uncooperative, which all but guarantees that it will not get a chance to come to a settlement or receive, if it needs to, leniency in sentencing or fines. But it goes far beyond that, Mr. Chairman. The uncooperative label can severely damage a company's brand, its shareholder value, [its] relationship with suppliers and customers, and [its] very ability to survive"); see

also, *Senate Hearings* (statement of Karen J. Mathis, President of the American Bar Association).

[126] *Id.*

[127] *Id.*

[128] *Id.*

[129] *Senate Hearing* (statement of Deputy Attorney General Paul J. McNulty).

[130] *Id.*

[131] *Id.* at 7.

[132] *House Hearing* 6 (testimony of Assoc. Attorney General Robert D. McCallum, Jr.)

[133] *Id.*

[134] *Senate Hearing* (statement of Deputy Attorney General Paul J. McNulty).

[135] 152 *Cong. Rec.* S11439, S11740 (daily eds. December 7 and 8, 2006).

[136] Department of Justice, *U.S. Deputy Attorney General Paul J. McNulty Revises Charging Guidelines for Prosecuting Corporate Fraud,* Press Release December 12, 2006, available at http://www.justice.gov/opa/pr/2006/December/ 06_odag_828.html.

[137] "... In conducting an investigation, determining whether to bring charges and negotiating plea agreements, prosecutors should consider the following factors in reaching a decision as to the proper treatment of a corporate target ... the corporation's timely and voluntary disclosure of wrongdoing and its willingness to cooperate in the investigation of its agents, *including, if necessary, the waiver of corporate attorney-client and work product protection* (see section VI, infra)," Thompson Memorandum, II.A.4 (language omitted in McNulty Memorandum in italics; see McNulty Memorandum, III.A.4).

[138] Holder and Thompson Memoranda, VI.B.

[139] *The McNulty Memorandum's Effect on the Right to Counsel in Corporate Investigations: Hearing Before the Subcomm. on Crime, Terrorism, and Homeland Security of the House Comm. on the Judiciary*, 110th Cong., 1st Sess. (2007)(House Hearings II); *Examining Approaches to Corporate Fraud Prosecutions and the Attorney-Client Privilege Under the McNulty Memorandum: Hearing Before the Senate Comm. on the Judiciary*, 110th Cong., 1st Sess. (2007)(Senate Hearings II).

[140] 153 *Cong. Rec.* S181-183 (daily ed. January 4, 2007)(text at S183).

[141] 154 *Cong. Rec.* S6294-295 (daily ed. June 26, 2008).

[142] The House Judiciary Committee reported H.R. 3013 without amendment, H.Rept. 110-445 (2007)(the text of the substance of the bill, *i.e.*, proposed 18 U.S.C. 3014, begins on page 8 of the report).

[143] 153 *Cong. Rec.* H13562-564 (daily ed. November 13, 2007)(text at H13563).

[144] Testimony of Deputy Assistant Attorney General Barry M. Sabin, House Hearings II at 14.

[145] Prepared Statement of Deputy Assistant Attorney General Barry M. Sabin, House Hearings II at 19-22.

[146] Testimony of Professor Michael Seigel, Senate Hearings II at 1. Since the relevant Senate hearings from the 110th Congress are not yet publicly available, the citations to Senate hearing testimony here and elsewhere refer to the pages in the witness's prepared statements available on November 16, 2007 at http://judiciary.senate.gov.

[147] Testimony of United States Attorney Karin Immergut, Senate Hearings II at 6.

[148] Testimony of Professor Daniel Richman, Senate Hearings II at 2; *see also*, Testimony of United States Attorney Karin Immergut, Senate Hearings II at 7.

[149] Testimony of Professor Michael Seigel, Senate Hearings II at 5-6 ("The bulk of that leverage, of course, would come from the threat of the ultimate sanction: termination. Only an employee truly mired in criminality would suffer this consequence rather than cooperate").

[150] Testimony of United States Attorney Karin Immergut, Senate Hearings II at 8.

[151] Testimony of American Bar Association President Karen J. Mathis, House Hearings II at 45; testimony of former Attorney General Dick Thornburgh, Senate Hearings II at 1-2; 153 *Cong. Rec.* H.13564 (daily ed. November 13, 2007)(American Bar Association letter in support of H.R. 3013).

[152] Testimony of William M. Sullivan, Jr., Esq., House Hearings II at 33-4; *see also*, *Restricting Prosecutors' Powers: Increasing Oversight to Reinstate Corporate Interests*, 92 IOWA LAW REVIEW 1523, 1548 (2007).

[153] Testimony of Andrew Weissmann, Esq., House Hearings II at 24; *see also*, Griffin, *Compelled Cooperation and the New Corporate Criminal Procedure*, 82 NEW YORK UNIVERSITY LAW REVIEW 311, 378 (2007)("Even setting aside whether the end of fighting corporate crime can be achieved via the Thompson and McNulty Memoranda, the means here violate important Fifth Amendment protections").

[154] Testimony of Andrew Weissmann, Esq., House Hearings II at 24-5.

[155] Statement of Richard T. White, Chairman of the Board of Directors of the Association of Corporate Counsel, House Hearings II at 89.

[156] Testimony of former Attorney General Dick Thornburgh, Senate Hearings II at 2.

[157] Testimony of Andrew Weissmann, Esq., Senate Hearings II at 4.

[158] Proposed 18 U.S.C. 3014(a)(3)("The term 'organization' does not include—(A) a continuing criminal enterprise, as defined in section 408 of the Controlled Substances Act (21 U.S.C. 848); (B) any group of individuals whose primary purpose is to obtain money through illegal acts; or (C) any terrorist organization, as defined in section 2339B").

[159] Proposed 18 U.S.C. 3014(b).

[160] Proposed 18 U.S.C. 3014(b)(2)("In any Federal investigation or criminal or civil enforcement matter, including any form of administrative proceeding or adjudication, an agent or attorney of the United States shall not consider any conduct described in subparagraph (B)[claiming attorney-client or work product privileges, paying attorneys' fees for employees, entering into joint defense agreements with employees, and refusing to fire employees who claim their constitutional or other rights] in—(i) making a civil or criminal charging or enforcement decision relating to an organization, or a current or former employee or agent of such organization; (ii) determining whether an organization, or a current or former employee or agent of such organization, is cooperating with the Government").

[161] Proposed 18 U.S.C. 3014(c)("Nothing in this section shall be construed to prohibit an agent or attorney fo the United States from requesting or seeking any communication or material that—(1) an agent or attorney of ordinary sense and understanding would not know is subject to a claim of attorney-client privilege or attorney work product; (2) an agent or attorney of ordinary sense and understanding would reasonably believe is not entitled to protection under the attorney-client privilege or attorney work product doctrine; or (3) would not be privileged from disclosure if demanded by a subpoena duces tecum issued by a court of the United States in aid of a grand jury investigation").

[162] Proposed 18 U.S.C. 3014(e).

[163] "Principles of Federal Prosecution of Business Organizations," Memorandum from Mark Filip, Deputy Attorney General to Heads of Department Components [and] United States Attorneys, dated August 28, 2008 (Filip Memorandum)(with U.S. Attorneys Manual, Title 9, Chapter 9-28.000 attached), available at http://www.justice.gov/dag/readingroom/dag-memo-08282008.pdf.

[164] Id.

[165] U.S. Attorneys Manual §9-28.710.

[166] U.S. Attorneys Manual §9-28.700.

[167] U.S. Attorneys Manual §9-28.720 ("so long as the corporation timely discloses relevant facts about the putative misconduct, the corporation may receive due credit for such cooperation, regardless of whether it chooses to waive privilege or work product protection in the process").

[168] U.S. Attorneys Manual §9-28.730.

[169] U.S. Attorneys Manual, §9-28.730.

[170] The superseded provision stated, "Another factor to be weighed by the prosecutor is whether the corporation, while purporting to cooperate, has engaged in conduct intended to impede the investigation (whether or not rising to the level of criminal obstruction). Examples of such conduct include: overly broad assertions of corporate representation of employees or former employees; overly broad or frivolous assertions of privilege to withhold the disclosure of relevant, non-privileged documents; inappropriate directions to employees or their counsel, such as directions not to cooperate openly and fully with the investigation including, for example, the direction to decline to be interviewed; making presentations or submissions that contain misleading assertions or omissions; incomplete or delayed production of records; and failure to promptly disclose illegal conduct known to the corporation," McNulty Memorandum, VII.B.4.

[171] Section 2(b) in both bills.

[172] Proposed 18 U.S.C. 3014(a)(1) in both bills.

[173] Proposed 18 U.S.C. 3014(a)(2) in both bills.

[174] S. 445, proposed 18 U.S.C. 3014(a)(3)(A) ("The term 'organization'—(A) means an organization as defined in section 18 of title 18, United States Code, and any State, local, or municipal government entity or instrumentality"). 18 U.S.C. 18 defines organization as "a person other than an individual." The Dictionary Act, which provides definitions applicable through out the Code unless the context dictates otherwise, provides that the word "person" includes "corporations, companies, associations, firms, partnerships, societies, and joint stock companies, as well as individuals," 1 U.S.C. 1.

[175] S. 445, proposed 18 U.S.C. 3014(a)(3)(B).

[176] Proposed 18 U.S.C. 3014(b) in both bills.

[177] Id.

[178] S. 445, proposed 18 U.S.C. 3014(b)(1)(B), (d).

[179] *Revisions of the Thompson Memorandum and Avoiding the Stein Problems: A Review of the Federal Policy on the Prosecution of Business Organizations*, 42 CONNECTICUT LAW REVIEW 273, 317-18 (2009).

[180] Proposed 18 U.S.C. 3014(c) in both bills.

[181] Proposed 18 U.S.C. 3014(d) in both bills.

[182] "This Act does not affect any other federal statute that *may* authorize[s], in the course of an examination or inspection, an agent or attorney of the United States to require or compel the production of attorney-client privilege material or attorney work product," proposed 18 U.S.C. 3014(e) in both bills; the italicized work "may" appears only in the Scott bill.

[183] *E.g.*, 42 U.S.C. 2996h(d)("Notwithstanding the provisions of this section or section 2996g of this title, neither the Corporation nor the Comptroller General shall have access to any reports or records subject to the attorney-client privilege"); 7 U.S.C. 2143(a)(6)(B) ("No rule, regulation, order, or part of this chapter shall be construed to require a research facility to disclose ... to the Institutional Animal Committee during its inspection, trade secrets or commercial or financial information which is privileged or confidential").

[184] Proposed 18 U.S.C. 3014(f) in both bills.

[185] *Prosecutorial Discretion of the Department of Justice in Corporate Criminal Cases*, 74 BROOKLYN LAW REVIEW 231, 270-71 (2008); see also, 155 *Cong. Rec.* S2331-332 (daily ed. Feb. 13, 2009)(remarks of Sen. Spector).

[186] *The Attorney-Client Privilege Protection Act: the Prospect of Congressional Intervention into the Department of Justice's Corporate Charging Policy*, 35 FORDHAM URBAN LAW JOURNAL 1075, 1136 (2008).

INDEX

#

20th century, 3, 13

A

ABA, 72
abuse, 17, 60
access, 14, 38, 62, 66, 81
accountability, 73
accounting, viii, 41, 42, 52, 54, 76
Administrative Office of the United States Courts, 75
advancement, 54, 59
affirming, 35
agencies, 57, 61, 64, 66, 74, 75
aid and abet, vii, 1, 6
ALI, 72
alters, 12
American Bar Association, 51, 75, 79, 80
antitrust, 17, 24, 35, 68
anxiety, 51
arraignment, 56
arrest, 7
articulation, 57
assessment, 20, 21, 55, 74
assets, 2, 17
attachment, 30
Attorney General, 27, 47, 59, 62, 72, 78, 79, 80
audit(s), 20, 22, 27, 39, 67, 74
authenticity, 50
authority(s), 3, 5, 7, 8, 10, 11, 19, 22, 27, 34, 36, 38, 39, 42, 43, 44, 55, 62, 65, 66, 68, 75
awareness, 7
Azerbaijan, 32

B

bargaining, 22
base, 18, 36
beneficiaries, 19
benefits, 26, 54, 58, 78
blogs, 29
blood, 68

C

case law, 16, 18, 68
challenges, 73
Chamber of Commerce, 30, 78
child pornography, 21
children, 22
City, 24, 35, 77
civil rights, 8, 24
classification, 28
clients, 44, 46, 78
co-conspirators, 6
coercion, 55

collateral, vii, 1, 9, 36, 59
commerce, 43, 64
commercial, 2, 13, 17, 31, 35, 81
common law, 2, 3, 24, 43, 44, 63
communication, 44, 69, 70, 75, 80
community, 20, 23, 37
community service, 20, 23, 37
compensation, 14
compliance, vii, 1, 9, 10, 11, 12, 18, 19, 20, 22, 28, 30, 36, 37, 38, 39, 45, 48, 49, 57, 68, 70, 73
compulsion, 6
confidentiality, 39, 46, 71
conflict, 15, 42, 70
confrontation, 16, 34
Congress, 1, 4, 6, 7, 24, 35, 42, 43, 52, 57, 58, 60, 62, 63, 66, 68, 69, 79
consent, 46, 68
conspiracy, 6, 7, 24, 26, 35, 68
Constitution, 12, 34
constitutional challenges, viii, 41
control group, 45, 70
Controlled Substances Act, 22, 80
controversial, 10, 52
conversations, 70
conviction, 2, 7, 8, 17, 20, 21, 24, 27, 34, 36, 37, 50, 76
cooperation, vii, 1, 9, 10, 17, 28, 36, 48, 49, 50, 53, 54, 61, 62, 74, 81
copyright, 21, 35
Corporate officers, vii, 1
corruption, 9, 19, 68
cost, 30, 77
counsel, viii, 2, 15, 29, 32, 33, 41, 45, 46, 48, 49, 52, 55, 56, 57, 59, 66, 69, 70, 71, 72, 78, 81
Court of Appeals, 45
covering, 58
crimes, vii, 1, 2, 3, 8, 17, 31, 36, 50, 66
criminal activity, 47, 73
criminal acts, 24, 67
criminal justice system, 27, 56
criminal statutes, vii, 3, 4, 43
criminality, 79
criticism, 65
CRM, 29, 30
culture, 22, 57, 66
cure, 56
customers, 78

D

damages, 24
danger, 7
death penalty, 35
debts, 26
defence, 53
defendants, vii, 1, 8, 13, 16, 22, 31, 33, 34, 36, 53, 55, 56, 77, 78
delegates, 27
denial, 32, 53
Department of Justice, 29, 30, 42, 66, 78, 79, 82
destruction, 27
detection, 36
deterrence, 20, 36
directives, 10, 20
directors, 25, 28, 29, 48
disclosure, 9, 17, 29, 36, 45, 46, 47, 48, 49, 50, 51, 57, 58, 59, 62, 69, 71, 74, 75, 79, 80, 81
discrimination, 32
disposition, 77
District of Columbia, 46, 77
DOJ, 29, 66, 67, 73, 74
domestic violence, 21
drug trafficking, 8
due process, viii, 2, 14, 15, 32, 33, 41, 52, 53, 54, 55, 76, 77

E

employees, vii, viii, 1, 2, 3, 5, 6, 8, 9, 10, 11, 12, 20, 22, 24, 25, 28, 29, 36, 39, 41, 42, 44, 45, 48, 49, 52, 53, 54, 55, 56, 57, 58, 59, 60, 61, 62, 63, 64, 65, 67, 68, 69, 70, 74, 77, 78, 80, 81
employers, 2
employment, 5, 24, 25, 44, 67, 68, 70

enforcement, 9, 11, 28, 45, 50, 56, 58, 59, 60, 61, 65, 74, 75, 80
England, 24
environment, 10, 19, 57, 60
equality, 13
ethical standards, 58
ethics, 18, 22, 37, 38, 39
evidence, 7, 8, 12, 16, 27, 34, 42, 73, 74, 77
execution, 26
exercise, viii, 8, 28, 32, 38, 41, 47, 58, 59, 65, 75, 76, 78
explosives, 35, 68
exposure, 50

F

fairness, 32, 60
fear, 39
federal authorities, 29, 58
federal courts, 13, 14, 42, 46
federal crimes, vii, 1, 66
federal district court, viii, 41
federal government, 14, 32
federal law, vii, 2, 3, 5, 6, 43, 63
federal prosecution, vii, 1, 8, 42
felon, 68
Fifth Amendment, viii, 2, 14, 15, 31, 32, 33, 41, 52, 53, 55, 60, 61, 77, 80
financial, 4, 29, 76, 78, 81
financial planning, 29
firearms, 35
First Amendment, 2, 13, 15, 30, 32
flavor, 17
flexibility, 50
flight, 22
food, 27
Fourteenth Amendment, 14, 32, 53, 76
Fourth Amendment, 2, 13, 31, 32
France, 25
fraud, 8, 21, 22, 29, 35, 36, 66
fraudulent tax shelters, viii, 42
funds, 56, 78

G

gambling, 17, 26, 29, 35
GAO, 29
Georgia, 33
good behavior, 12
governments, 14
grand jury, 14, 27, 31, 62, 66, 80
gravity, 16
grouping, 35
guidance, 28, 39, 50
guidelines, vii, viii, 1, 8, 9, 10, 11, 12, 28, 35, 41, 47, 50, 51, 72
guilt, 16, 24, 49, 78
guilty, vii, 2, 7, 11, 24, 29, 49, 60

H

Harvard Law School, 29
hazardous materials, 22
history, vii, 1, 9, 17, 36, 47, 73
House, 28, 29, 42, 51, 57, 60, 62, 63, 66, 67, 75, 78, 79, 80
human, 4, 21, 34, 64, 77
human dignity, 77

I

ideal, 32
identification, 35
identity, 33
immigration, 8
immunity, 31, 43, 48, 72
imprisonment, 29, 31
improvements, 61
inadmissible, 55
independence, 30
individuals, 2, 4, 6, 7, 12, 13, 16, 17, 18, 26, 31, 32, 33, 34, 36, 38, 43, 44, 70, 73, 80, 81
industry, 31, 60
information sharing, 64
inhibition, 7
initiation, 56

injury, 19
innocence, 25, 78
insider trading, 35
inspections, 13, 31
inspectors, 66
integrity, 16
interference, 22, 54, 61, 71, 78
Internal Revenue Service, 45
Interstate Commerce Commission, 24
intervention, 56
issues, vii, 42, 77

J

Japan, 30
joint stock company, 24
joint-stock companies, 4
Judicial Conference of the United States, 75
judiciary, 79
Judiciary Committee, 42, 51, 57, 60, 79
jurisdiction, 11, 14, 27, 32, 68
Justice Department, vii, viii, 1, 3, 8, 10, 41, 42, 50, 57, 61, 64, 66, 72, 73
justification, 60

L

law enforcement, 10, 58
laws, 2, 12, 14, 27, 29, 32, 33, 58, 68
lawyers, 70
Leahy, 75
legal issues, 77
legal protection, 63
legislation, vii, 7, 42, 70
legislative proposals, 60, 61
liberty, 14, 53, 76
LIFE, 67
light, 19, 34, 44, 63, 67, 70, 77
litigation, 42, 44, 46, 52, 58, 63, 71
local government, 19, 75
Louisiana, 33

M

mail fraud, 36
majority, 43
malfeasance, 3
management, 5, 9, 22, 69
marketing, viii, 41
marketplace, 75
materials, 31, 63, 65, 71
matter, 6, 21, 22, 25, 27, 34, 35, 42, 43, 44, 46, 50, 55, 70, 76, 78, 80
meat, 27
Medicaid, 36
medical, 21
mental processes, 46
mental state, 26
microscope, 53
misconduct, vii, 1, 5, 6, 7, 9, 10, 11, 17, 18, 19, 20, 22, 24, 28, 30, 36, 42, 43, 44, 46, 49, 53, 74, 81
mission, 10
modifications, 39
money laundering, 35, 36
multiplier, 36

N

national security, 19
negotiating, 79
negotiation, 12
New England, 25

O

obstruction, 7, 9, 10, 36, 49, 54, 63, 81
officials, 5, 6, 10, 11, 26, 45, 57
omission, 25, 64
operations, 22, 25
organizational culture, 38
oversight, 12, 38

P

Pacific, 32
parallel, 33
penalties, 30
permit, 19, 48, 51, 66
perpetrators, vii, 1
Philadelphia, 33, 77
Philippines, 71
piracy, 22
police, 68
policy, viii, 41, 42, 45, 51, 52, 56, 57, 59, 60, 61, 66, 70, 73, 75, 76
predictability, 75
prejudice, 15, 53, 56
preparation, 71
president, 26, 27, 78, 80
prima facie, 7
principles, 28, 44, 57, 58, 63, 75
probability, 7
probe, 67
profit, 10, 61
program features, 22
proposition, 30, 67
prosecutorial discretion, vii, 27, 41, 44, 47, 58, 59, 73, 75
protection, 2, 13, 14, 15, 26, 28, 31, 32, 33, 42, 44, 46, 47, 51, 53, 57, 58, 59, 61, 62, 64, 65, 69, 71, 74, 75, 76, 79, 80, 81
public interest, 29, 44
public policy, 3, 43
public welfare, 7
punishment, 2, 7, 12, 17, 20, 34, 36, 43, 68

Q

questionnaire, 69
Qwest, 71

R

race, 28
racketeering, 4, 35, 36, 68
reading, 28, 45, 64
reality, 57
recognition, 24, 60
recommendations, 30, 74
regulations, 24
regulatory agencies, 50
reliability, 34
relief, 52
religion, 28
remedial actions, 48
remediation, 74
requirements, 7, 18, 20, 31, 70
resolution, 3, 12, 30, 70, 74
resources, 30, 38, 54, 77
response, 9, 21, 31, 65, 67, 70
restitution, vii, 1, 2, 9, 10, 17, 18, 20, 21, 22, 30, 34, 37, 38
restrictions, 13, 14, 53
retaliation, 39
RICO, 24, 64
right to life, 53
rights, 2, 8, 10, 12, 13, 14, 15, 16, 28, 32, 33, 43, 52, 55, 61, 63, 77, 78, 80
risk(s), 19, 20, 39, 42, 49, 78
rules, 12, 42, 67, 68, 71, 75, 76

S

safety, 24
sanctions, 11, 17, 23, 28, 29, 60, 74
school, 31
scope, 5, 24, 25, 31, 44, 50, 62, 64, 65, 67, 68, 70
securities, 2, 30
Securities Exchange Act, 74
seizure, 13, 31
self-incrimination, viii, 2, 14, 31, 41, 52, 55, 77
Senate, 28, 57, 60, 67, 78, 79, 80
Senate Committee on the Judiciary, 67, 78
sentencing, 2, 17, 18, 20, 22, 28, 34, 35, 51, 72, 78
Sentencing Guidelines, vii, 2, 3, 10, 17, 28, 35, 51, 52, 73, 74
services, 29, 56, 69, 76
sexual abuse, 21

shareholder value, 78
shareholders, 11, 20
shelter, 30
Sherman Act, 24
shock, 55, 77
smuggling, 17, 35
society, 33, 78
sole proprietor, 28
South Dakota, 32
speech, 2, 13, 30, 72
stability, 66
state(s), 5, 12, 14, 16, 26, 32, 33, 49, 51, 56, 64, 66, 67, 75, 76
statutes, 4, 5, 7, 23, 34, 43, 62, 65, 66
statutory authority, 60, 66
stock, 4, 43, 81
stockholders, 19
structure, 9
subpoena, 2, 31, 62, 66, 67, 80
Sun, 24
supervision, 45
supervisor, 75
suppliers, 78
suppression, 55
Supreme Court, 3, 7, 13, 14, 15, 16, 31, 32, 43, 45, 46, 56, 67, 76
survival, 71

T

target, 79
Task Force, 75
tax evasion, 35
taxes, 35
telemarketing, 21
tenure, 30
territorial, 68
terrorist organization, 64, 80
terrorists, 61, 64
The Justice Department, vii, 8, 41, 57, 73
theft, 21, 35
tobacco, 35
Toyota, 26
trade, 81
traditions, 61
trafficking, 21, 22
training, 20, 38
training programs, 38
transactions, 35, 43
transportation, 22, 43, 68
treatment, 20, 55, 73, 79
trial, vii, 1, 2, 7, 11, 12, 15, 16, 33, 34, 71
trust fund, 23

U

unions, 16
United, viii, 6, 14, 23, 24, 25, 26, 27, 28, 29, 30, 31, 33, 34, 35, 36, 39, 42, 43, 44, 49, 51, 59, 63, 65, 67, 68, 69, 70, 71, 72, 73, 74, 75, 76, 77, 78, 79, 80, 81
United States, viii, 6, 14, 23, 24, 25, 26, 27, 28, 29, 30, 31, 33, 34, 35, 36, 39, 42, 43, 44, 49, 51, 59, 63, 65, 67, 68, 69, 70, 71, 72, 73, 74, 75, 76, 77, 78, 79, 80, 81
unreasonable searches, 2, 13, 30, 31, 32
USA, 23, 25, 30, 31

V

venue, 16
victims, 19, 34, 36, 53, 56
violence, 21
vulnerability, 18

W

waiver, 10, 28, 42, 46, 47, 48, 49, 51, 52, 57, 58, 59, 60, 61, 65, 66, 67, 71, 74, 75, 79
Washington, 76
wealth, 57
wire fraud, 36
Wisconsin, 77
witnesses, 2, 15, 16, 33, 34, 48, 57, 60
wrongdoing, 7, 9, 42, 47, 50, 53, 57, 76, 79